The Great
Piano Virtuosos
Of Our Time

In memory of Philip Reder

Wilhelm von Lenz

The Great Piano Virtuosos Of Our Time

Edited by Philip Reder

Kahn & Averill, London

Published in association with
Kensington Chimes Music Ltd

First published in German in 1872
First English edition published by Schirmers of New York in 1899
This edition first published by Kahn & Averill in 1983
Copyright © 1983 by Philip Reder

British Library Cataloguing in Publication Data

Lenz, Wilhelm von
  The great piano virtuosos of our time
  1. Pianists — Biographies
  I. Title
  786.1'092'2   ML397

  ISBN 0-900707-77-1

Printed and bound in Great Britain at
The Camelot Press Ltd, Southampton

Contents

Introduction

Wilhelm von Lenz (1809–1883) was not a great musicologist — neither was he a great writer. At best he was a devoted amateur — a dilettante of enthusiasm and charm, who was lucky enough to come into contact with such great masters as Chopin and Liszt. Von Lenz may well have been bitterly disappointed could he have known that his more serious (and much lengthier) works were to be overshadowed by his brief accounts of his meetings with Liszt, Chopin, Tausig and Henselt. His "Beethoven et son trois styles" was published in 1852 (in two volumes), in which he deals in depth with the idea suggested by Fétis that Beethoven's works could be divided into three distinct periods. Later there appeared (in six volumes) "Beethoven — eine Kunststudie", a work more enthusiastic than scholarly. But his "Die Grossen Pianovirtuosen unserer Zeit", originally published a century ago, has a charm and simplicity — and brevity — quite different from what von Lenz considered his more important work.

Here we find portraits of Liszt, Chopin, Tausig, and Henselt that remind us that they were not only musical geniuses, but human, too. And they were not only great piano virtuosos, but great artists as well. Their thundering fortissimos were to be matched by their delicate and subtle pianissimos. It was not only showmanship. Tausig, in spite of his keyboard fireworks, despised "Spectakel". And what Calvocoressi wrote in his preface to "Beethoven et son trois styles" is as true today as it was then. Liszt knew it. And Tausig knew it. But not all pianists know it.

"Aujourd'hui on ne joue plus le piano, on le monte. Devenu cheval de cirque, de fougueux et intrepides cavaliers promenant ce pauvre piano aux yeux d'un public ébahi, à tant de notes par minute, et tous d'applaudir. On monte le piano sellé ou non sellé".*

---

* Today people no longer play the piano, they ride it. It has become a circus horse, the poor piano, which dashing and intrepid riders put through its paces before an astonished audience, at so many notes a minute; and everyone applauds. One rides the piano saddled or not.

LISZT, FRANZ. 1811–1886.

I Franz Liszt

I was personally acquainted with all the great pianists of the first half of the century: John Field, Moscheles, Hummel, Kalkbrenner. Now we call this the "old" school (with the exception of Field, who developed in his own peculiar way) — a school of piano-playing which if not founded by Hummel, was at least essentially influenced by him, and led to the new era of the pianoforte, to Liszt and Chopin.

Liszt is a phenomenon of musical virtuosity such as has never been seen before. He is not merely a pianistic wonder. Liszt is a phenomenon spreading over the whole domain of music, and creating a universal standard of comparison.

Liszt does not just play the piano; he tells at the piano, the story of his own destiny, which is linked to, and reflects, the progress of our time. Liszt is a latent history of the keyboard — its crowning glory. To him the piano becomes an expression of his highest mental cultivation, of his faith and being. What does "piano-playing" matter to him! Of him, one should say, "Climb the tower, and see how the battle goes" — how far enquiry has reached into the domains of science, how far speculation has fathomed musical thought, how does it go on in the world of intellect — that is what one has to learn from his playing (how else were such playing possible?) and to learn for the first time, for one could never go so far alone.

His desire to become a priest came from the innermost core of his being. It was thematic. The "man-of-the-world" in Liszt is but an episode from the theme. For the priest alone are the portals of infinity the home of the soul. Priest in continuation of Prophet; and Liszt was ever a prophet from the beginning of his career.

When Liszt thunders, lightens, sighs on the piano that "Song of Songs" — the great B flat major Sonata (The Hammerclavier) by Beethoven, he coins capital for mankind out of the ideas of the greatest musical thinker that the world has ever known. Beethoven himself could have had no conception of such a rendering of the "Hammerclavier".

The pianist in Liszt is an apparition not to be compressed within the bounds drawn by schools and professors. The old proverb applies: "Quod licet Jovi, non licit bovi". (What Jove can do, the bull cannot.)

Nothing could be more foolish than to attempt to imitate Liszt, or even to use him as a standard by which to criticise others. Where Liszt appears, all other pianists disappear; there remains only the piano, and that trembles in its whole body!

Liszt is the past, the present, the future of the piano. He is the spirit of the matter; he absorbs the conception. How can the perishable hope to compete with the imperishable? This entire pianistic stronghold is the material side of the matter, however much spirit might have occupied the guest chamber. One cannot suspend a ghost as a barometer in the sitting-room! So Liszt is no pattern, but the beginning, continuation, and end. Hence in Liszt's case, any comparison with any given performance at the piano is a priori out of the question. He is the exception, because he is the prophet who ceased to be a plain citizen, in order to become a soldier of the spirit in his own church, his own ideas. Such an intellect must be rated as higher than a piano. It is an accidental circumstance, of no importance, that Liszt happens to play the piano at all. Perhaps in a higher sense, this is not the case, but the piano being merely visible, like the "tub" in Mesmer's case. It is altogether uncritical to say that Liszt does this or that differently from somebody else. Do not imagine that Liszt does anything — he "does" nothing at all; he "thinks", and what he thinks takes on this form. That is the process. Can it really be called piano-playing? Liszt, then, cannot be expected to practise scales and finger exercises, as is the custom among schools and professors. Does the eagle practise flying? He looks upwards, gazes towards the sun, unfolds his pinions, and soars towards its burning light!

I will describe the circumstances which brought me to Liszt, since one makes the acquaintance of such a spirit in no ordinary way. One gains access to him, or one does not. That is the whole matter, and signifies much in either case.

In 1828 (forty-three years ago!) I was nineteen years old. I had come to Paris to continue my studies on a broader scale, and to take piano lessons (as people used to say) with Kalkbrenner. Kalkbrenner came from Berlin, of Jewish extraction. In Paris he was the "Joconde" of the salon-piano, under Charles the Tenth. He was a knight of the Legion of Honour, and farmer-general of all permissible pianistic elegancies. The beautiful Camille Mock, who later became Mme. Pleyel, and to whose charms neither Liszt nor Chopin was indifferent, was the favourite pupil of the irresistible Kalkbrenner. I once heard her play — together with Kalkbrenner and Onslow — the latter's Sextet from manuscript. This was at the home of Baron Trémont, a tame musical Maecenas of the time. She played the piano as one would wear an elegant shoe, when one is a pretty Parisienne. Nevertheless, I was in danger of becoming Kalkbrenner's pupil, but Liszt and my good star ordered it otherwise. On the way to Kalkbrenner (who plays a note of his, nowadays?), as I was walking along the boulevards, I read among the theatre posters of the day, which exercised so powerful an attraction, the notice of an "additional" concert (it was already November) to be given at the Conservatoire by Monsieur Liszt. Beethoven's E flat major Piano Concerto headed the programme.

Beethoven was then (and not only in Paris) Paracelsus personified, in the concert-room. Of Beethoven, at that time, I knew only that I had been frightened by his ladder-like notes in the D major Trio, and in the Fantasia with chorus, which I had once opened (and immediately closed) in a music shop in my native city, Riga, where more was doing in trade than in music.

How astonished I would have been if somebody had told me, as I innocently stood before the advertising-column in Paris, and learned from the notice that Beethoven had written such things as piano concertos, that some time in the future I should write six volumes in German, and two in French, about Beethoven!

From the notice I concluded that anybody who could play in public a piano concerto by Beethoven must be a remarkable person, and quite different from Kalkbrenner, the composer of the Fantasia Effusio Musica. That this Effusio was a trumpery piece, I already understood — young and happy though I was.

It was in this manner — on the fateful Paris boulevards — that I first saw the name of Liszt, which was to fill the world; — on the boulevards where one fancies one is contributing to the daily history of

Europe when one takes a walk!

That concert notice was to have a lasting influence on my life. Even after all these years, I can see the colour of that fateful paper — gigantic black letters on a bright yellow background — the colour that was all the rage in Paris in those days.

I drove straight to Schlesingers in the Rue Richelieu, whose place was at that time the musical exchange of Paris.

"Where does M'sieur Liszt live?" I demanded, and pronounced it "Litz", for the Parisians never got further with Liszt than Litz. (That good German Rudolf Kreutzer, who happened at the time to be the best violin virtuoso in Paris, they called "Kretch", whereupon the man to whom Beethovem had dedicated his great Op. 47 violin sonata, had his cards engraved: "Rudolf Kreutzer, prononcez Bertrand".)

Liszt's address was Rue Montholon, far away, where Paris imagines she has become a mountain! What has not Paris imagined — and what have we ever refused to believe of her? Mountain and valley, Heaven and Hell — all these has she imagined herself to be.

They gave me Liszt's address at Schlesingers without any hesitation, but when I asked how much he charged for lessons, and made known my wish to study with Litz, they all laughed at me, and the clerks behind the desk giggled with them, and they all said at once: "*He* has never given a lesson — he is no piano teacher!" I felt that I must have said something very stupid, but the reply "He is no piano-teacher" pleased me, and I made my way directly to Rue Montholon.

Liszt was at home. That was a very unusual thing, his mother told me — an excellent woman with a German heart, who pleased me extremely. Her Franz was almost always at Church, she said, and — "busied himself no more with music!" Those were the days when Liszt wished to become a Saint Simonist; when Pére Enfantin infested Paris; when Lamennais wrote the "Paroles d'un Croyant", and the "Peau de chagrin" of Balzac followed close upon his "Scènes de la vie privée".

It was a grand epoch, and Paris was the centre of the earth. Rossini lived there, and Cherubini, also Auber, Halévy, Berlioz, and the great violinist Baillot, and Victor Hugo, who was later to be banished for political reasons, had published his "Orientales", and Lamartine was just recovering from the exertions of his "Méditations poétiques". We were soon to be in the midst of the July revolution, but we were still under the Martignac ministry.

Odilon-Barrot spoke "con sordini" in the Chamber, Cuvier lectured in the Jardin des Plantes, Guizot and Villemain in the Sorbonne; Cousin had discovered philosophy: Lerminier — Savigny and Ganz — one ran from one to the other! Scribe was doing his turn at the Théâtre, where Mlle. Mars was still playing. Dumas had given his best piece, "Henry III et la Cour" at the Theatre Français, where the first performance was repressed by the ministry because there was something in it about "Lilies". Paris prided itself upon possessing both the Classic and the Romantic Schools, and these factions were at daggers drawn. There were masked balls at the court of Charles X, at which the Duchesse de Berry appeared as Mary Stuart, the Duc de Chartres as Francis I. The Duchesse de Berry's lovely foot was much talked of, and Salvandy said — at the Duc d'Orléans' ball in the Palais Royal — "We are dancing on a volcano". George Sand was not yet well known — Chopin not yet in Paris. Marie Taglioni danced at the Grand Opéra, and Habenek, a German master, conducted the Élite Orchestre at the Conservatoire — where the Parisians, one year after Beethoven's death, heard for the first time, some of his music. Malibran and Sontag sang the "tourney" duet in "Tancredi", at the Italian Opera. It was the winter of 1828–1829; Baillot played in quartets and Rossini was to present his "William Tell" in the New Year.

In Liszt I found a pale, haggard young man, with unspeakably attractive features. He was reclining on a broad sofa, smoking a long Turkish pipe, and apparently lost in deep meditation. Three pianos stood near. He made not the slightest sign when I entered — he did not even seem to notice me.

When I explained to him, in French — at that time no one presumed to address him in any other language — that my family had sent me to Kalkbrenner, but that I had come to him because he dared to play a Beethoven concerto in public — he seemed to smile. His smile, however, was like the glitter of a dagger in the sunlight.

"Play me something", he said, with indescribable sarcasm, which nevertheless, did not hurt my feelings — any more, for instance, than one feels insulted when it thunders.

"I will play the Kalkbrenner Sonata for the left hand", said I, feeling that I had chosen well.

"That I will not hear. I do not know it, and I do not care to know it!" he answered with even stronger sarcasm, and hardly concealed scorn.

I felt that I was making a very poor impression. Perhaps I was expiating the sins of someone else, of some Parisian. However, I said to myself, as I looked at this young Parisian — for in appearance at least he was thoroughly Parisian — that he must surely be a genius, and thus, without any further skirmishing, I did not care to be driven from the field by any Parisian. With modest, but firm step, I approached the nearest piano.

"Not that one!" cried Liszt, without in the least changing his half-recumbent position on the sofa, "There, at the other one."

I walked to the second piano. At that time I was absorbed in Weber's "Invitation to the Dance." I had married it out of pure love two years before, and we were still on our honeymoon. I came from Riga, where the unparalleled success of "Der Freischütz" had prepared the way for Weber's piano music, while in Paris "Der Freischütz" was called "Robin (!) des bois", and was embellished by Berlioz with recitative!

I had studied with good masters. But when I tried to strike the three first A flats, I found it quite impossible to make the instrument give forth a sound! What was the matter? I struck hard. The A flat sounded — but quite piano. I must have seemed to be very foolish — I felt sure of that — but without losing courage, I went straight on to the entry of the first chord — then Liszt got up, came over to me, pulled my right hand off the keyboard, and asked: "What is that? That begins well!"

"I should think it does", I replied, with the pride of a parish clerk for his pastor. "That is by Weber".

"Has he written for the piano, too?" he asked, astounded. "Here we know only his "Robin des bois!"

"Certainly he has written for the piano, and more beautifully than anyone else", was my equally surprised answer. "I carry in my trunk" I continued, "two Polonaises, two Rondos, four sets of Variations, and four Sonatas. I studied one of these Sonatas with Vehrstaedt in Geneva. It contains the whole of Switzerland in it, and it is inexpressibly beautiful. In it, all lovely women smile at once. It is in A flat major. You can't imagine how beautiful it is. Nobody has written anything to compare with it for the piano, believe me".

I spoke from the heart, and so convincingly that

Liszt was strongly impressed.

There was silence for a few moments, and then he said in his most winning tone: "Please bring me everything you have in your trunk, and for the first time in my life, I will give lessons — to you — because you have introduced me to Weber's piano music, and because you did not allow yourself to be discouraged by the stiff action of this piano. I ordered it so myself. One scale played on such a piano is equal to ten on any other! It is a completely impossible piano. It is a "mauvaise plaisanterie" on my part. But why did you speak of Kalkbrenner and his Sonata for the left hand? But now, play me your piece which begins so curiously. That piano you first tried is one of the finest instruments in Paris".

Then I played the "Invitation" most enthusiastically — but only the "Cantilena" section, marked "wiegend" (swaying, rocking) in two parts. Liszt was charmed with the composition. "You must bring me that", he said. "We will interpret it to each other". Thus the last letter of the alphabet came to the first.

In our first lesson Liszt could hardly tear himself away from the piece. He played through the different parts over and over again. He tried various reinforcements. He played the second part of the minor movement in octaves, and was inexhaustible in his praise of Weber. And what, indeed, did one find in the piano repertoire at that time? The bland master-joiner Hummel; Herz, Kalkbrenner, and Moscheles — nothing plastic, dramatic, or speaking, for the piano. Beethoven was not yet understood. Of his thirty-two piano Sonatas, only three were to be heard — the A flat Sonata with the variations (Op.26), the C sharp minor quasi Fantasia, and the Sonata in F minor, which a publisher's fancy — not Beethoven — christened "Appassionata". The five last Sonatas were still considered monstrous abortions of a German idealist who did not understand how to write for the piano. People understood only Hummel and Co. Mozart was too old-fashioned, and in any case did not write such passages as Herz, Kalkbrenner, Moscheles — to say nothing of the lesser lights.

In the midst of this Flowery Kingdom dwelt Liszt, and one must take this into account, in order to grasp the greatness of the man who discovered Weber and his own genius at the piano when he was scarcely twenty years old.

Liszt was altogether enraptured with Weber's A flat major Sonata. I had studied it in Geneva with Vehrstaedt, and expressed in my interpretation the true spirit of the composition. Liszt proved this to me by the way he listened, by his gestures, by his exclamations of approval. We were as one man in our adoration for Weber.

This great romantic poem for the piano begins with a tremolo in the bass, on A flat. No Sonata ever began that way before. It is like the sunrise over an enchanted forest where the action takes place. Liszt's restlessness over the first part of the first Allegro became so great, that before I came to the close, he pushed me aside, saying: "Wait — wait! What is that? I must play that myself!" He played it, and I had never heard anything like that! Think of a genius like Liszt, but twenty years old, coming into contact, for the first time, with such a magnificent composition — with that apparition of that Knight in Golden Armour, Weber!

He played the first part over and over again in various ways. At the section (in the dominant) in E flat at the close of the first part, he said: "It is marked legato there. Would it not be better to make it pianissimo and staccato? Leggermente is indicated there, too". He experimented in every direction.

So I had the experience of observing how one genius looks upon the work of another, and turns it to his own account.

"Now, how is the second part of the first Allegro?" asked Liszt, as he examined it. It seemed to me quite impossible that any one could read this part at sight, where the theme is carried in crowded octaves, several pages long.

"This is very hard", said Liszt, "and the coda is still harder. To hold the whole piece together in this centrifugal figure (thirteen bars from the end) is most difficult of all. This passage in the second part — of course in the principal key, A flat, we will not play staccato — that would be rather affected. Neither will we play it legato — that is too thin. We will make it spiccato — let us swim between the two waters".

If I admired the spiritual passion, the fire and the life in Liszt's rendering of the first movement, in the second part I was even more astounded by his confident repose and certainty, by the way in which he held himself back so as to reserve his strength for the last attack. So young, and so wise! I felt disheartened and discouraged.

I learned more from Liszt in the first four bars of the Andante of that Sonata, than I had learned in years from my earlier teachers!

"This exposition is to be in the manner of Baillot when he plays in quartet, the accompanying parts are in the lifted semi-quavers. But Baillot's parts are very good. You must not make yours inferior to his. You have a good hand — you can learn it. But take care — it is not easy. One can move stones with that. I can imagine how the piano-hussars will charge through it! I shall never forget that I became acquainted with this Sonata through you. Well, in return you shall learn something from me. I will tell you everything I know about our instrument".

The demi-semi-quaver figure in the bass of the Andante (bar 35) one too often hears played merely as a passage for the left hand. It should be played caressingly — a violoncello solo, "con amore". So Liszt played it. But with what terrible majesty he played the octave eruption upon the second theme in C, which Henselt calls the "Ten Commandments" — a capital title.

How can I begin to express what Liszt did with the Minuetto Capriccioso, and the Rondo of the Sonata, the very first time he saw these inspired compositions? What was there *not* in his treatment of the clarinet solo in the trio of the Minuet, the modulation of that cry of longing, the winding ornamentation of the Rondo!

After considering the composer's genius of handling the piano, and of writing for it, one might confidently say of the Weber Sonatas that as specific piano music, they leave the Beethoven Sonatas behind — although not as musical ideas for which the piano is the medium of expression. The Mozart Sonatas are sketches for quartets; Beethoven's Sonatas are symphonic rhapsodies. But the noble Weber Sonatas are the happiest expression of the piano, in its most happy mood. The piano writing of Weber is quite free of quartet or symphony. It is self-dependent, self-sufficient, conscious *piano*, and opened the door to the New School — to the treatment of the instrument by Liszt and Chopin.

And has there ever been manifested greater genius in the handling of the piano, than is found in Weber's *first* Sonata — the one in C major? One is astounded by this work of the year 1813, when it was severely criticised by that great blind woman the "Allgemeine musikalische Zeitung". It may yet have been written earlier — a work which emancipated itself from the forms which controlled musical thought for sixty years. In Art, we do not part the spirit from the form. The paternal home, the hearth, the household altar — these are the motives of the Weber C major Sonata. The youthful soul finds expression for its impulse towards the unknown country which lies beyond the narrow precincts of his homely native town. This longing supplied Weber with words for his sonata-poem in C: "Vom Mädchen reisst sich stolz der Knabe". (From the arms of the maiden, he proudly tears himself away) is the clear meaning of the diminished chord at the beginning, through which Weber's poem rushes into life. The Weber Sonatas unite us to life. Beethoven's relation to life — at the piano — is that of the preacher to the parish.

The world knows, and future generations will talk about for years to come, of Liszt's magnificent interpretation of Weber's piano compositions — and especially of the "Concertstück".

I now come to a thought which I fancy is original, since nobody else has spoken of it. It explains Liszt's wonderful way of writing for the piano as arising from esoteric causes, and gives to his technical difficulties an extremely artificial appearance. I regard Liszt's style of writing for the piano as a satire on the distinctions of rank, the conventionalities and absurdities of the early Parisian salons, which, in their pitiful puerility through three different forms of Parisian government, I had opportunity to observe. These weak pretentions of every sort constituted the difference between France and Germany, and between France and the freer atmosphere of St. Petersburg, where the artist, as the epitome of culture, is equal in rank to the highest-born in the land. In Paris, the relation of the artist to the world around him, turns rather in the opposite direction, and this condition of affairs is not always conducive to his happiness. The difficulties of Liszt's style are — so to speak — variations on his own Parisian theme: "Stirb, vogel, oder friss!" (Die, bird, or eat).

Liszt tossed these technical difficulties in the faces of the Parisians. "I require no thanks, ladies", he says. "Do this after me", he says. "Who and what are you" he says. He who did not live in Paris was not considered to be living at all. Of this city, Liszt was at the same time the scourge and the darling. His method, hard to describe, is an expression of his unparalleled pianistic technique, and it would be a mistake to suppose that anyone could ever approach such individuality, no matter how thoroughly he might overcome the difficulties of his piano writing. Let all composers assemble, and each orchestrate the simple chord of C major. Beethoven's chord would be Beethoven. And that is the heart of the matter. So it is with Liszt. Let all pianists come together and attack the E flat piano Concerto of Beethoven. Liszt's first chord will betray the fact that it is he, and no other! His imagination, his conception, his fantasy is imponderable. It is disembodied. All other pianists are lost in the shadow cast by Liszt. He is a doctor, like Faust, and we are his Wagner.

Since one has to go to Rome in order to *see* Liszt — to say nothing at all about *hearing* him — ever since Liszt turned his back upon the public, one can speak only of *having* heard him, and must no longer refer to him as a *pianist*. Liszt is like a dead man, who is fortunately still alive — a pianist he is not. In his personality, he is an image of our day, in which more happens than formerly took place in a century. Quite apart from his musical supremacy, Liszt is one of the great intellects of the century.

As for the explanation and the proper view of Liszt's manner of writing; of himself, of his genius, I would say: "Art is the ideal Truth of earthly life. She is the disembodied Truth. Art can exhibit herself in many ways. The difficulties of Liszt are nothing external — they are the key to his inmost being."

CHOPIN, FRÉDÉRIC FRANCOIS. 1810–1849

II   Frédéric Chopin

Europe, from Madrid to St. Petersburg was lionizing Liszt, when, in 1842, we again found ourselves in Paris, where now Louis Philippe had become King. Twelve years had passed since the year 1830, when the French nation hung upon the word of the Citizen King. It was, nevertheless a great and stirring time — a time of ideas — and Paris, through the influence she exercised on manners and customs — but still more through the belief, universally shared, in her dictatorial supremacy — was the central Sun in the constellation of Europe.

Life had become elegantly frivolous, whereas under Charles X it had been simply corrupt. Then, Vice had worn its livery. Now it was transformed into a sort of "demi-monde", with all sorts of socially acceptable titles, with the accepted grades of "Duchesse", "Camélia", etc.

At that time Thiers lived in the parish of the church of Notre Dame de Lorettes, Place St. George, in the pleasant hôtel of his mother-in-law, Madame Deaune, with a small garden next to the street. He was, from time to time, minister to King Louis Philippe — though this did not amount to much — and never lasted long. Thiers certainly did not then believe that a Revolution would find it worthwhile to raze his house to the ground, or that he, the little Advocate from Marseilles, was destined to rise on the ruins as President of the French Republic!

At that time — 1842 — George Sand was an established fact. The whole range of Camélia literature was in full bloom. Balzac thought that Paris breathed an electric atmosphere. Paris, and Paris alone, was where one could live.

And there lived Chopin. Just now, however, in the month of August, he was still in Touraine with George Sand, living in a château of too diminutive proportions to be called a "castle". In truth, the spirit of the time, and of the Pleiades of Art and Literature which it produced, was manifested in the wish to appear greater than one actually was, and to spend what one did not have! The term "distinguished" (le distingué) was the fashion, and went through the most fantastic gradations. To return to Paris before the month of November — or far worse, to shut oneself up in Paris all through the summer, was not "distinguished". And Chopin was *very* distinguished — not like the dead-and-gone Kalkbrenner, as a peacock or a silver pheasant (neither was he decorated with even the smallest Legion of Honour ribbon), but as a great artist, albeit a good, fashionable Parisian, was Chopin distinguished. In his easy, well-bred reserve, in his manners, in his very appearance, he sought to be, and was, distinguished.

This time I did not travel to Paris from Riga, via Geneva, but I came direct from St. Petersburg. Since the A flat major Weber Sonata, I had passed fourteen years in St. Petersburg, *quantum mutatus ab illo*! (How much changed from what he was.) Liszt, too, was back in Paris, fresh from his spectacular and

magnificent triumph in St. Petersburg, where he, alone
and unaccompanied, appeared before four thousand
people in the Hall of the Nobility. Women of the
highest rank waited for him on the steps of his hotel,
with garlands of flowers. The greatest nobles secured a
steamboat, with choruses of singers to accompany the
great artist as far as Kronstadt, and even further — to
the roadstead of the Gulf of Finland, when he set sail
for Germany.

My first visit in Paris was to Liszt, who lived now in
Rue Blanche, not far from our Rue Montholon of
1828. The mother of the great artist again received me
most kindly, but she did not tell me, as she used to,
that I "wearied her Franz" and that he was always in "a
dreadful state" after I, with my Weber Sonatas, had
been to see him. Her Franz no longer attended church
so assiduously. He carried his church within himself,
and no longer wished to become a St. Simonist.

Liszt himself received me royally. His first words
were: "I shall go to see you every day, since you live so
conveniently near Schlesinger, where I go so often. I
shall send you an Érard grand, and, at the instrument,
we will live over again the good old times — especially
the Weber Sonatas. I suppose you have them with
you?"

"In the same copy", I replied, "with your notes,
which I keep as a holy relic. But I should like some
Chopin."

"We will study whatever you like", said Liszt.
"Only don't dare to imagine that you are to pay me.
For no price would I give lessons. I shall be visiting a
friend; all I ask is a cup of coffee from the hotel. I will
come every day, promptly at two o'clock, and we will
meet only in the afternoon and evening, for you must
spend the entire morning at the piano. I shall send you
the very best instrument. I shall go myself to Érard's

and select one".

Those were afternoons never to be forgotten! Liszt seldom missed the hour — another sign of his unfailing politeness. I see him now, standing in the doorway of my hotel, his hat on his head, an elegant Verdier stick in his hand, his spiritual, expressive countenance laughing up at me! I felt that I had been made king in Paris.

Once I played him his own arrangement of Schubert's "Ständchen". "Give me a pencil", said he, and wrote in it: *"Comme naturaliste, parfait"*, and signed with his crooked signature: *Franz Liszt*. "How *naturaliste*", I objected, "when I have you for a teacher?" "Well", he replied, "you play it very well. You play it heartily — very heartily, and quite faultlessly. But you do not play it like a virtuoso, and only a virtuoso (and not many of them) can play the Coda as I wish. It is devilishly hard — not just the notes, but the piece as a whole, and in virtuoso-like expression. That is what I mean".

Next I played him Weber's Polacca in E. "Here is more work for a virtuoso", he said. "You play it very well, but you have not sufficient strength for it.. You must have the devil in you to play that". I played the "Moonlight Trio". "That you play very well", said Liszt. "That is perfect — give me the pencil"; and he wrote in it: "Ceci est parfait". "Do you see, this is the antidote for the Schubert! Where did you learn that fingering? That change from the thumb to the second finger, and back again (in the dotted middle part on B and E)? That is not your own invention. It is good, but a little choppy — one might come to a standstill. Whose fingering is it?"

"It is by Moscheles in London — in the time after you, in 1829".

"Oho! Was he so learned in Weber, then? Now *I*

will play *you* the Polacca. It will be better".

When he left, I always went as far as the courtyard with him, and as he went down the winding stairs he repeated several times: "That Trio was capital — capital. You had not practised it, had you? It is very difficult, this *cantilena*; one does not get it from one's so-called strong pupils, and here in Paris, never. So, keep to Weber. That is your native soil".

Then I was happy, and began to consider myself a "foudre de guerre" at the piano! How happy one can become, with a little conceit! Those were blessed days — those days of the Weber alliance with Liszt!

Since then, Liszt has been happily inspired to combine the serious and striking Introduction of Weber's first and insignificant Polacca in E flat, with the noble E major Polacca, and to arrange the whole for piano and orchestra, and thus to honour the virtuoso repertoire with an inestimable gift. The connecting passage between the Weber Introduction and the Weber Polacca, composed by Liszt, is the most intelligent and tasteful piece of work one can imagine. It is like a beautiful face whose expression reveals the soul of romance. It is like the enchanted wood of Titania in the midst of other forests. It is inimitably conceived. Chopin would have wept over it. He never soared so high. He never rose to the romantic — he remained poetically material. He sat, a prisoner of the conventional atmosphere of Paris.

One morning Liszt said: "It is fine weather — let us go for a walk — but what kind of a great-coat are you wearing?"

"A sort of brown velvet tiger-skin", I replied. "I bought it in Hamburg, and it fits beautifully".

"In Paris, it will only make you conspicuous. I am the only man in Paris who would dare give you his arm, whilst you wear that Hanseatic pelt! Come, we will have some macaroni at Broschi's, opposite the Grand Opera. Rossini goes there — we will sit at his table".

As we walked along the Boulevards, and as I noticed how curiously people looked at us, I understood Liszt's remark that he alone would dare show himself with someone wearing such a coat. Chopin would never have done it — it might have displeased the Sand! How strange, affected, and small the city of Paris was — and ever will be!

We come again to Weber's A flat Sonata in its turn. "Very good, very good", said Liszt, when I played the Rondo — "but still not enough of the Countess B . . . in St. Petersburg. The eloquent foot is not there". He played the foot. I studied, and played through the Rondo again under his hawk-eyes. "Now it is much better", he said. "The foot is there but where is the shoe?" He played the shoe. Thus he always had to say and do something, and he was always right. It was the passage in the Rondo, beginning at the twenty-fourth bar, with the serpentine scales in the bass in F minor. Liszt forgot it long ago, in Rome. But I shall remember it all my life.

In Chopin's B flat major and A minor Mazurkas, Op.7, I learned a great deal about piano-playing in general from Liszt. In both pieces he put in important little variations from what was printed, taking the matter very seriously, especially in the apparently so easy bass in the major section of the A minor Mazurka. What pains he took with me there! "Only an idiot", he said, "would think that was easy. In this phrasing you recognise the virtuoso. Play it thus to Chopin, and he will notice something. He will be pleased. These stupid French editions bungle everything of his. These slurs must run *so* in the bass". Liszt played it, and marked in the slurs. "If you play like that to him", he said, "he will give you lessons. But you must have courage to do it".

It was already October, but Chopin was so disting-uished that he was not yet in Paris. But one morning Liszt said to me: "Now he is coming. I feel sure of it, if the Sand will only let him go". I said: "If *he* would only let *her* go!"

"That he will never do, Liszt replied. "I know that. When he is here I will bring him to you directly; after all, you have the Érard. We shall play, as if by chance the Onslow four-hand Sonata duet in F minor, that you are so fond of. He and I once played it in Paris, in public. Strangely enough, Chopin played the *primo* — but that was my idea! He'll be glad to do it again. You must get the Sonata. Get it at Schlesinger's, and make sure it's in the Leipzig edition — that is the correct one. In that way you'll get lessons from Chopin. It will arrange itself — you'll see — especially in the beginning of the season. You don't know Paris yet — you can't imagine how difficult it is to have lessons with Chopin. With me, it is nothing. But hard — so hard — with Chopin! Many have journeyed all the way to Paris, and have not been able even to get a glimpse of him".

From that time I walked on air in Paris. To dare to hope that Liszt and Chopin would play in *my* apartments! I was greeted in front of the music shops. Every time I went into Schlesinger's, I was offered a chair — for had I not passed with Liszt? At Schlesin-ger's I met Berlioz. He understood little of piano-music, and looked — in his blue frock-coat with brass buttons, and decorated with his well-earned Legion of Honour — like a musical Robert Macaire (a character whom Frédéric Lemaître exhibited at the Theatre of the Port St. Martin). Berlioz called Liszt "le cher sublime", which was considered very spiritual! People in those days were regularly astonished when anyone dared to clamber over the hedge of conventional speech.

When I next met Berlioz, in 1868 in St. Petersburg, after the death of his only son, his hope and joy, he looked like the Vicar of Wakefield at a funeral. It was no use then talking to him of Liszt. He had come to consider the B flat Symphony of Beethoven the greatest of them all! There lay the poor suffering man, always on his back, in the palace of the Grand-Duchess Helena, where he was living. There at his bedside, I read to him reports of the concert, directed by him, and given, under the patronage of the Grand-Duchess, by the Russian Musical Society. There he gave me, at parting, his daguerreotype, on which he wrote with his own hand: "A l'homme qui a sû aimer et admirer! Son frère dévoué, Hector Berlioz". Berlioz was unhappier than King Lear!

October came, but still no Chopin. With much difficulty, and some inconvenience, I managed to obtain an extension of my leave from St. Petersburg. I waited patiently, and was as diligent as possible at my Érard. I continually practised the "volate" that Liszt had noted for me in the Chopin B flat major Mazurka — so as to "keep my right hand in". The particular point was this: instead of returning to the theme, from F to F (an octave lower), to go two octaves higher, and then fall back into the lower octave — that is, to take twelve F's in triplets, and on no account to miss coming in exactly on time. Under Liszt's hand, this was a rocket with its returning shower of stars, in the reprise of the theme.

I mention this in order to warn adepts never to presume to attempt anything like it. These naïve mistakes always mislead, and make one appear as ridiculous as a German who tries to speak French (to quote Goethe).

One evening Liszt came to see me, with the excellent pianist Ferdinand Hiller, and the famous violin virtuoso, Ernst. The *good* piano was at my lodgings, and plenty of music to hand. Liszt and Hiller together played the overture to "Der Freischütz," and Ernst fiddled with them with might and main. The idea had come into their heads that afternoon, and Ernst had brought his violin along. They remained for the evening, and "made jokes of all kinds", as Liszt put it. "Where does Cramer live?" I asked. "He has founded a Lancaster Pianoforte School", replied Liszt. "You cannot see him — he is never in the city. He lives in the suburb of Batignolles".

Cramer, who had made a lot of money in London, had speculated through a banker, and lost everything. He had become an Englishman in England, and had now come to Paris, which did not suit him at all. "Cramer is a septuagenarian", said Liszt. "Leave him alone. From him you can learn nothing, since you have *me*".

But I did not leave Cramer alone. To me he was sanctified, *venerabilis Beda*! I remember having heard him at a concert at the Argyle Rooms in London, in 1829. He played magnificently — the E flat Piano Quartet of Mozart, with his brother, Franz Cramer playing the violin, and Lindley the well-known English violoncellist. I wrote Cramer a respectful letter reminding him of this occasion, and mentioning Count Wielhorski, who had met him in Rome, and told me much about him. That was the connecting link. The author of the world-renowned Études — that hymn-book of unconfirmed pianists — wrote back, promising to come. "Now", I said to myself, "we will order an English dinner — all the dishes to be served at once, the best port, and all his works on the table!" Schlesingers sent me his complete works — a huge pile

CRAMER, JOHANN BAPTIST. 1771–1858

of music, which must have been covered with a layer of dust an inch thick — but they were in good condition. They contained the history of a whole human life.

I drove about the whole day in order to procure a first-class English meal, and port wine. This was far from easy in such a singular place as Paris. Unfortunately Liszt had left Paris. He would not have refused to play some Cramer from that pile! That would have been an event, indeed!

Cramer arrived on the stroke of seven — he had written earlier to say that he would "not be out of school earlier!" I could hardly believe my eyes. From as long as I could remember, Cramer had stood in a holy shrine at Riga, and here he stood bodily before me! I kissed his hand. He was embarrassed, but it seemed to me the only thing to do. "I have but this to offer you", said I and led him towards the pile of his assembled works.

"Are all those mine?" he sighed. "Have I written all that? And who plays it now? But I am glad, I am very glad", and he shook me by the hand in the English fashion. We spoke in French — English seemed out of place unless Cramer began, and German is not a language suitable to Paris.

Dinner was served — everything English, even the plates. He noticed it at once. "Do you live in the English fashion?" he asked in surprise. "It is a little attention to you", I replied, and that seemed to please him. "There was a time when I drank such wine", he said, as he tasted the port. "But where did you find it, here in Paris?" He went on: "There is said to be only one place where you can find good port in Paris and that is at the 'Trois Têtes de Mores'. It is an American firm! Strange city, this Paris, is it not? I do not like it — I would have done better had I gone to Germany. But here the climate agrees with me. I have been here for some years, and I am too old now to go further".

Cramer was sparing of words, and his replies were always quiet and deliberate. When I asked him about Chopin, he said: "I do not understand his music, but he plays beautifully and correctly — oh, so correctly! He does not allow himself to become careless like so many other young people. But I do not understand him. Liszt, of course, is a phenomenon, and he does not always play his own compositions like Chopin. As for this modern music, I do not understand it!"

The atmosphere over dinner was depressing. Why? It seemed to me that Cramer would cling so closely to the past, that the present had no interest for him. I, sitting opposite him, and already thirty-three years old, seemed so young and insignificant. After dinner, however, he became more talkative. I went over to the Érard, and asked him to allow me to play to him his first three studies. He sat down at my side, and thus, I might say, I took lessons with Jean Baptiste Cramer!

I should never have dreamed, in my younger days, that such things were possible. Vehrstaedt of Geneva, used to play the Études in concerts. With him, I studied the third D major, with its intricate fingering, its careful slurring, and rich "cantilena", like a prayer, or slumber-song. Cramer said: "From me you have nothing to learn. These are only exercises. Do you actually play such things for pleasure?" "Indeed I do!" I replied, and I opened with the Étude in F with the triplet figure in quavers. "See what a beautiful 'pastor-ale' this is", and I told him of Henselt in St. Petersburg, who played this Étude so wonderfully. This pleased him, and at my request, he played the first three Études. It was dry, wooden, harsh, and there was no "cantilena" in the D major Étude, although it was rounded and masterly. The impression I received was painful in the extreme. Could this indeed be Cramer?

Had the great man lived so long, only to remain so far behind the times? I did my best not to show my feelings, but I had lost my bearings, and could think of nothing to say. I asked whether he did not think an absolute legato was indicated in the third Étude. He had so cut off the notes in the upper part, and so ignored the phrasing of the bass, that I could hardly believe my eyes and ears. Cramer answered: "We were not so particular. They are only studies; we did not consider them of great importance. I do not have your modern accents and fancies. Clementi played his 'Gradus ad Parnassum' just so, and it was good enough for us. Nobody has ever sung so beautifully on the piano as John Field, and he was a pupil of Clementi. My pattern was Mozart. No one has ever composed better than he. Now I am forgotten. I am only a poor teacher of rudiments in a suburb of Paris, where they study only the Bertini Études. I must even teach Bertini myself! You can hear it any time — eight pianos, all going at once!"

I spoke of Hummel, who dedicated his Piano Trio in E major to Cramer. I said that I thought the first part fine, but it develops into nothing more than smooth passages.

"Next to Mozart, Hummel is the greatest composer for the piano", said Cramer. "No one has surpassed him". I knew that Cramer could not stand Beethoven, let alone Weber! I had removed all my music from the room so that nothing remained except the works of J.B. Cramer. I brought out his four-hand Sonata in G (the one with the Adagio in C). I had loved to play it with my life-long friend Dinglestaedt, in the happy days of my youth. Cramer wondered that I should know it. He had to look at it very carefully himself before he played it — and then he played the bass part so roughly and clumsily, that all that remained to me was the honour of having sat next to the composer! I had only once before in my life suffered so great a disenchantment from so famous an artist. That was in the summer of 1827, in Frankfort-on-Main, when I heard Beethoven's pupil, Ferdinand Ries. He, too, was a woodchopper at the piano.

Cramer was thick-set, with a full, ruddy countenance and dark brown eyes. He looked like an Englishman, and he had English manners, and considering his age, he was very vigorous. "I am a good walker", he said. "I walked all the way from Batignolles to Paris". He stayed late into the evening, sorting out some of his oldest compositions, and playing parts of them. "I don't remember that! I don't know this any more", were his words. I listened with the greatest reverence, but could not approve of his treatment of the piano. It was repulsive. When he left, he said: "Receive the blessing of an old man — I owe you an evening such as I thought never to enjoy again. I sincerely hope that it may bring you happiness. And so you say, I am not altogether forgotten?" I told him: "In St. Petersburg the great virtuoso Henselt plays your Études in concerts. In my native city, Riga, the Études lie upon every piano — they rank with Bach's "48" as a Book of Wisdom. They have never been equalled, and like Bach's work, they can never be laid aside!"

I spoke from my heart. That Cramer had visited me, I could, and still can hardly believe. The worthy man died a few years later, in poverty, and forgotten by all. That would never have have been the case had he lived in Germany! Cramer is a poet and an artist in his Études.

In the meantime, Meyerbeer had arrived in Paris, and was at work on his new opera, the name of which he refused to tell anyone. It was "L'Africaine". His arrival was something of an event in Paris.

Liszt had left his visiting card with me, on which he wrote the following words for Chopin: "Laissez passer, Franz Liszt". He said to me; "Present this at Chopin's. Without it you may never succeed in seeing him at all. You must have a 'laissez passer' — that is the custom among authors and artists of the first rank — we cannot afford to lose our time. About two o'clock in the afternoon, go to the Cité d'Orléans, where he lives, and where also live the Sand, the Viardot, and Dantan" — (the famous cartoonist, who had drawn a caricature of Liszt playing the piano with *four* hands). "In the evening, all these people assemble at the house of a Spanish countess — a political refugee. Perhaps Chopin will take you there. But do not ask him to introduce you to the Sand — he is very mistrustful!"

"He has not your courage, then?"

"No, he has not, poor Frédéric!"

At last I could go to Chopin.

The Cité d'Orléans was a new district of large proportions, with a spacious court — the first of its kind — and a number of apartments, with numbers, and a name (Cité), is always popular with Parisians. It lay behind the Rue de Provence, one of the fashionable quarters of Paris. It looked — as indeed it was — aristocratic.

I gave Liszt's card to the man-servant in the ante-room. A man-servant is an article of luxury in Paris, and very rarely to be found in the home of an artist! The servant said that Chopin was not in Paris — but I did not allow this to deter me. "Deliver this card", I said, "and I will attend to the rest". Chopin soon came out, the card in his hand. He was a young man — not very tall — slim, and haggard, with a sad, but most expressive face, and elegant Parisian bearing. I have seldom, if ever, met with an apparition so entirely engaging. He did not ask me to sit down. I stood before him as if I were before a monarch. "What do you wish? Are you a pupil of Liszt? An Artist?" I replied: "A friend of Liszt. I wish to have the privilege of studying with you your Mazurkas, which I regard as a Literature. I have already studied several of them with Liszt". I felt that I had been somewhat indiscreet, but it was too late.

"So?" said Chopin, very deliberately, but still in a most amiable tone. "Why, then, do you need me? Play me, if you please, those you have studied with Liszt". He drew an elegant little watch from his pocket. "I still have a few minutes. I was going out — I had forbidden the door to anyone — you must pardon me". I found myself in the same painful situation that I had been thirteen years earlier, with Liszt — another examination! After Liszt, however, I felt that I need fear no one, and without further ado, I went straight to the piano, and opened it as if I was quite at home. It was a Pleyel; I had been told that Chopin never used any other instrument. The Pleyel has an easier action than that of any other Parisian manufacturer. I struck a chord before seating myself, to get the depth of touch ('le gué', I called it). This, and my manner, seemed to please Chopin. He smiled, and leaned wearily against the piano, and his keen eyes looked me directly in the face. I dared only one glance towards him, then taking my courage in both hands, I started the B flat major Mazurka — the typical one, to which Liszt had given me the variants.

I played it well. The "volata" through the two octaves went better than ever before, and the instrument was easier to the touch than my Érard. Chopin whispered engagingly: "That little bit is not your own, is it? *He* showed you that! *He* must have his hand in everything! Well, he may dare. He plays to thousands,

I seldom to one! Very well, I will give you lessons. But only twice a week — that is the most I ever give. It will be difficult to find three-quarters of an hour". He again looked at his watch. "What books do you read? How do you occupy yourself in general?" That was a question I was well prepared for. "I prefer George Sand and Jean Jaques to all other writers", I said, too quickly! He laughed — he was beautiful at that moment. "Liszt told you to say that — I see you are initiated. So much the better. But you must be very punctual. With me everything goes by the clock — my house is like a dovecot. I see already that we shall get on together — a recommendation from Liszt means something. You are the first pupil he has recommended to me. We shall be friends — we shall be comrades".

I always went to him long before my lesson was due, and waited in the ante-chamber. One lady after another came out — each one more beautiful than the last. Once it was Mlle. Laure Duperré, the Admiral's daughter. She was a most lovely woman, tall and straight, like a palm tree; Chopin always accompanied her to the stairs. To her he dedicated two of his most important Nocturnes (C minor and F sharp minor, Op.48). She was, at that time, his favourite pupil. In the ante-room I often met little Filtsch. He was only thirteen years old — a Hungarian genius. He understood, and how he played Chopin! At a soirée at the house of the Duchesse d'Agoult, Liszt said of Filtsch, in my presence: "When this little one goes on the road, I shall shut up shop!" I was jealous of Filtsch, for Chopin had eyes only for him. He gave him the B flat minor Scherzo (Op.31), after he had refused to allow me to learn it, saying it was too difficult for me. He was right, too. But he allowed me to stay when Filtsch played it, so I have often heard this wonderful work at its very best. Filtsch also played the E minor Concerto, which Chopin accompanied himself at the second piano, and insisted that Filtsch played it better than he. I did not believe it. Perhaps Chopin had little strength, but nobody could approach him in grace and elegance, and when he embellished, it was always the apotheosis of good taste. In his earlier days, Chopin had given concerts, and won a reputation for himself in Paris as high as that of Liszt. That is saying a great deal. Now he played only once a year, semi-publicly, to a select circle of his pupils and friends — amongst them the flower of the highest society, who took tickets in advance, and divided them among themselves, as he told me.

"Do you practise on the day of the concert?" I asked him.

"It is a terrible time for me", he replied. "I do not like the publicity, but it is a duty I owe to my position. For two weeks I shut myself up, and play Bach. That is my preparation. I do not practise my own compositions".

Chopin was the Phoenix of intimacy with the piano. In his Nocturnes and Mazurkas he is unrivalled, unbelievable. His Mazurkas are the songs of Heine on the piano. When I told him so, he played in an abstractedly sort of way with the chain of his little watch, which he always kept on the piano during lesson time so as not to overstep the three-quarters of an hour, which always passed so quickly with him. "Yes, you understand me", he said. "I listen with pleasure when you play something of mine for the first time, for then you give me ideas. If you prepare yourself, it is not at all the same. It becomes mediocre". "Liszt said the same thing to me". I blurted it out before I could stop myself.

"Then I do not wonder that you agree with me", was his piquant and piqued rejoinder. With Liszt and

Chopin, one had to be extremely careful, for in point of sensibility, they were both very, very French. "Speaking of the Mazurkas", I said, "Liszt said you must harness a new pianist of the first rank to each one of them".

"Liszt is always right", said Chopin. "Do you imagine that I am satisfied with my own interpretation of the Mazurkas? A few times, I have been satisfied — in those early concerts, when I could feel the appreciative atmosphere of the audience. Only *there* must I be heard. The rest of the year is for work! There is that Valse mélancolique (the Waltz in A minor). You will never in your life be able to play it, but because you understand the piece, I will write something in it for you". And in my copy he altered the D and G sharp in the upper part of the eighth bar, to G sharp and C.

Chopin's autographs are rare; he wrote no letters, no notes. He was once heard to say: "George Sand writes so beautifully, that no one else has any need to write!" He went as far as that! How prone is Genius to be deluded by a woman! How far higher Chopin stood than George Sand! Chopin will still be played when not a single line of George Sand will be read! What has this woman, so over-rated in France, written? Chopin's works will always belong to the very finest literature of the piano, but the works of George Sand reflect only the decline of morals, and thus they are the reverse of good literature. Chopin was dazzled and blinded from the first for the poisonous plant, perhaps because only one side of his literary taste had been cultivated, not *all* sides, as was the case with Liszt. Such is often the case, and the English judge was quite right when he asked in every criminal case: "Where is the woman? I don't see the woman".

I managed with Chopin as one would manage with a woman whom one wished, above all things, to please.

With Liszt it was all the other way round — he managed me, and did just exactly as he pleased. Chopin once said to me, in one of his confidential moods: "I have only one fault to find with you — you are a Russian!" Liszt would never have said that. It was one-sided, it was narrow; but it was a key to his nature. He often made indirect excuses to me. Once he said: "It is good if one understands Beethoven and Weber so. No Frenchman ever can!"

I asked him one day if we might go and see Duperré. "Ah!" he said, "so *she* pleases you! I introduce no one. You have nothing to learn from her. You play my works in the style of Weber, and you have learned something from Liszt". Liszt would not have answered like that. He would have said: "When do you wish to go?" However, Chopin added, by way of excuse, "In a few days I must play the A flat Sonata of Beethoven (Op.26) to some Russian ladies. I have promised to do so. I pray you, come with me — it will be pleasant for me to have you. The ladies will send their carriage for me, and we shall drive in style — like princes". Carriages played an important part in the social life of this city — even in this circle!

The Russian ladies turned out to be the beautiful Baroness Krüdner, and her charming friend, the Countess Schérémetjew. I had known them both well in St. Petersburg, where they had never failed to be present at Henselt's Sunday afternoon matinées, and all the other musicales at the home of Count Wielhorski.

As we drove along the Boulevards, I spoke to Chopin of Henselt. "He would be glad to hear you", I said. "And I no less glad to hear him", replied Chopin. "Will he not come here sometime?" One must always *come* — the Parisians never *went*!

The Baroness' talented daughter was a pupil of Chopin, also the young Princess Tchernischov, daughter of the Russian Minister of War. It was to her that Chopin dedicated his C sharp minor Prelude, Op.45.

As we rolled over the Boulevards in the luxurious St. Petersburg calèche with liveried servants (to whom Chopin did not fail to draw my attention), I thought to myself: "This will not happen again — the first and last letters of the musical alphabet sitting side by side in the brilliant sunshine of beautiful Paris!"

Chopin had been sent for to play the Beethoven Sonata — the variation movement. How did Chopin play it? He played it well — but not so well as he played his own compositions. It was neat, but there were no contrasts, and certainly not like a romance, building up from variation to variation. His *mezzo voce* was a whisper, but his *cantabile* was unapproachable — perfectly finished, ideally beautiful, but womanish! Beethoven is a man, and never ceases to be a man. Chopin played on a Pleyel. At one time he would never give a lesson on any other instrument — one *had* to have a Pleyel. Every one was charmed. I, too, was charmed, but only by his tone, his exquisite touch, his grace and elegance, and by his absolutely pure style. As we drove back. I was absolutely frank and sincere when he asked my opinion. "I indicate", he said, without any touchiness; "the listener must finish the picture".

When we got back to his house, he went into a small room which adjoined the drawing-room, in order to change his clothes. I seated myself at the Pleyel. I felt that I owed something to Liszt, and I played the Beethoven theme so as to express an Autumn landscape, with a dash of summer sunlight! I made a special point of the three well-graduated crescendos, very intensive, in the five consecutive A flats (semi-quaver groups). Everything that was in it came forth, even to the sudden halt before the demi-semi-quaver group.

Chopin came at once, still in his shirt-sleeves, and sat down at my side. I played well — it was a sort of challenge, although not intentionally so. After the theme, I stopped and looked at him. He laid his hand on my shoulder, and said: "I will tell Liszt. It never occurred to me to play it like that, but it is fine. But must one always speak with so much passion?" I replied: "It is no drawing-room piece; it is the life of a human being. Rochlitz has written a novel about it. And that it must be played with passion is indicated in the coda of the last variation, where the B flats are only an accompaniment to the Aspiration, and are no longer dotted, and are played in the middle. But how wonderfully you play the triplets in the last variation! If only I could learn that of you! But it would be impossible — it is part of your nature. It is your way of playing the piano".

For the first time, we talked at length about Beethoven. He never cared very much for Beethoven. He knew only his great compositions, although of his later ones, nothing at all. The "Morin Quartet Society" had not yet been formed. Paris was always decades behind Germany.

I told Chopin, among other things, that in the F minor Quartet, Beethoven had foreshadowed Mendelssohn, Schumann, and Chopin himself; that the Scherzos prepared one for his own Mazurka Fantasias; that this did not mean that he had borrowed from Beethoven, but that Beethoven embraced all within himself. A universal genius like that, anticipates future epochs. "Bring me that Quartet", said Chopin. "I do not know it". I brought it, and he thanked me repeatedly. I brought him Weber, too, but he did not appreciate that. He spoke of opera as "bad piano-style". In general, Chopin was far from understanding the German spirit in music, although I heard him say more than once: "There is but one school — the German". The construction of his compositions is German, not French. He bears Bach in mind. Take, for example, the two C sharp minor Mazurkas, Op.50 and Op.4. They begin as though written for the organ, but end in an exclusive salon! They are in imitative style, and they do him much credit. They are more fully worked out than usual — they are sonnets as none of the others are. Chopin was pleased when I told him that in the structure of the Op.50 Mazurka, the passage from E major to F major was the same as that in the "Agatha" Aria from "Robin des bois". "I do not know the Aria, although I have heard it — show it to me", he said. I brought it to him, together with the C major Sonata, so that he could compare, too, the Trio of the Minuet, in E major, eight bars before the end. Chopin was delighted with it. "I didn't know anything like this had ever been written", he said. "And think how long ago Weber wrote them", I replied. "The Sonata in 1813, and 'Freischütz' in 1820!"

I tormented Chopin with the famous E flat major Nocturne, Op.9, which he dedicated to the lovely Camille Pleyel. He, like Liszt, was very sensible to the charms of women.

A Nocturne is simply a perfected Field, grafted onto a more interesting bass. In 1842 it was in the height of fashion. Now it is superseded by the more mature forms in Chopin — more especially in the C minor and F sharp minor Nocturnes, Op.48, which he wrote for Mlle. Duperré.

When Chopin was pleased with a pupil, he would make a small cross under the composition, with his small well-sharpened pencil. I had received one in the E flat Nocturne, my 'premier chevron'. Next time I came with it, I got another. I brought it a third time. "Do please let me alone", said Chopin. "I do not even like the piece. There! you have another cross. More than three I never give — you cannot do it any better!" "You play it so beautifully", I said. "Can no one else?" "Liszt can!" said Chopin, drily — and he played it to me no more. He had put in my copy some very important little changes. His notes were very clean, small and sharp, like English diamond type.

Dantan, George Sand, Pauline Viardot, Chopin, all lived in the Cité d'Orleans. They assembled in the evening at the same house, in the apartment of an old Spanish Countess, a political emigrée. All this I learned from Liszt. On one occasion Chopin took me with him. On the stairs he said: "You must play something — but nothing of mine. Play your Weber piece — 'The Invitation'".

George Sand said not a word when Chopin introduced me. That was hardly civil of her, and for that reason I immediately sat down close to her. Chopin hovered round like a frightened bird in a cage — he knew that something was coming. Was there ever a time when he was without apprehension in her presence? At the first pause in the conversation, which was conducted almost entirely by Sand's friend, Madame Viardot (I was later to become much better acquainted with this great singer in St. Petersburg), Chopin took me by the arm, and led me to the piano. If you are a pianist, you can imagine how sorely I stood in need of courage! It was a Pleyel upright, which in Paris passed for a pianoforte. I played the 'Invitation' somewhat fragmentarily. Chopin shook me by the hand; George Sand did not say a word. I sat down at her side again, and followed my purpose openly. Chopin looked at us apprehensively, across the table, on which the inevitable 'carcel' was burning. "Will you not come to St. Petersburg sometime?" I said, in my politest manner, to George Sand, "where you are read so much, and so highly respected". "I will never lower myself to visit a country where slavery still exists", she answered shortly. This was indecent, after she had been discourteous. "Well", I replied in the same tone, "perhaps you are wise not to come. You might find the door closed against you! I just thought of Kaiser Nikolaus". George Sand looked at me, astounded. I looked steadily back, into her beautiful, big, cow-like eyes. Chopin did not look at all displeased, Instead of answering me, George Sand rose, and strode across the room, like a man, and sat down at the glowing fire. I followed at her heels, and ready primed for the next encounter, sat down beside her. She had to say something, at last. She drew from her apron pocket an enormously thick Trabucco cigar, and called back into the drawing-room: "Frédéric, a light!" I felt insulted for him — my great lord and master. I understood Liszt's remark "Poor Frédéric!" in all its bearings.

Chopin obediently brought a light.

After the first abominable whiff of smoke, George Sand turned to me, and favoured me with a question. "I suppose", she said, "I could not even smoke a cigar in a drawing-room in St. Petersburg?" "In *no* drawing-room Madame, have I ever seen a cigar smoked", I answered with a bow. She looked at me sharply — the thrust had gone home! I looked quietly round at the fine pictures, each lit by a separate lamp. Chopin had returned to the table where our hostess sat, and had probably not overheard us. Poor Frédéric — how sorry I was for him — the great artist!

The next day, the 'porter' of my hotel, whose name was M. Armand, said to me: "A lady and gentleman have been here to see you. I told them you were not at home — you did not say you wished to receive visitors. The gentleman had no card, but left his name". I read: 'Chopin et Madame George Sand'. I quarrelled every day for two months with M. Armand. Such are the

Parisians. You must know beforehand if you are to have visitors, and it nearly always happens that visitors come at such inconvenient times that you have to be 'not at home'. It would have been an interesting visit. Chopin might even have played for me — I would have made him.

Chopin said to me during my next lesson: "George Sand went with me to see you. What a pity you were not at home. I regretted it very much. She felt she had been rude to you. You would have seen how amiable she could be — you pleased her very much!" The Spanish Countess probably had a hand in that visit. She was a well-bred woman, and she might have reproved George Sand for her rudeness to me. I drove to call upon George Sand; she was not in. I asked the concièrge: "What is Madame properly called — George Sand, or Madame Dudevant?" "Ah, Monsieur, she has many names", was the answer.

From that time on, Chopin was particularly pleasant towards me — I had pleased George Sand! That was truly a diploma. George Sand had actually considered me worthy of the honour of a visit! This was promotion, indeed! "You are accepted", Liszt had said to me a few weeks before, referring to a Parisian lady of the highest rank, whom he had always wished (and always succeeded) to please. But all I had done on that occasion was to tell the lady of Liszt's triumph in St. Petersburg, a thing he could not very well do himself. The following incident is entirely characteristic of Liszt. After I had told the above-mentioned lady the story of Liszt's triumph, she invited me — simply out of courtesy — to play Weber to her. Liszt found me still at the piano. He said: "So, in addition, you replace me at the piano, also!" He half spoke in jest, and half in earnest, as he always did, and indeed, as it was with everything in Paris!

I have already touched upon the altogether charming — but not *great* style of Chopin's playing. His playing, for example, of the so called Waltzes (they are really enchanted rondos of a kind hitherto unknown), is altogether inimitable. Once Meyerbeer came in whilst I was having a lesson with Chopin. I had never seen him before; he came in unannounced — he was a king! I was just playing the C major Mazurka (Op.33) — such a very short one, with so much in it. I called it the "Epitaph of the Idea", for it was so full of grief and sorrow — the weary flight of an eagle.

Meyerbeer sat down and listened, and Chopin allowed me to play on. "That is two-four time", said Meyerbeer. In reply, Chopin told me to repeat it, and kept time by tapping loudly upon the instrument with his pencil. His eyes glowed. "Two-four", repeated Meyerbeer quietly. I only once, in all the time I knew him, saw Chopin angry. A delicate flush covered his pale cheeks — he looked very handsome. "It is three-four", he said loudly — he who always spoke so soft! "Let me use it", said Meyerbeer, "as a ballet for my opera. Then I will show you". (He was writing 'L'Africaine', then kept secret). "It is three-four", Chopin almost screamed, and he played it himself. He played it several times, counting loudly, and stamping the time with his foot in rage! It was no use. Meyerbeer insisted it was two-four. They parted not on the best terms! It was anything but agreeable to me to have been present at this little scene. Chopin disappeared into his room, without saying a word, leaving me alone with Meyerbeer. The whole thing had only lasted a few minutes. I introduced myself to Meyerbeer as a friend of his friend Count Wielhorski in St. Petersburg. I walked with him down to the court, where his coupé awaited him. "May I take you home?" he kindly asked. No sooner were we seated when he began: "I had not seen Chopin for a long time — I love him dearly! There is no pianist like him. Nobody can compose for the piano like him. The piano is made for his delicate shading, for his 'cantilena'; it is the instrument for close intimacy. I, too, was a pianist once, and there was a time when I even hoped to become a virtuoso. When you are in Berlin you must come and visit me. We are comrades — when two people meet under the roof of such a great man it is for life". Meyerbeer spoke in German, and so heartily! He pleased me far more than the Parisians. But all the same, Chopin was right. Though the third beat in the Mazurka is slurred over, it certainly exists — but I took care not to press this point with the composer of 'Les Huguenots'!

Twenty years later, I met Meyerbeer again, in Berlin. His first words were: "Do you remember? It was during your lesson that I interrupted". I replied: "You hurt his feelings. What must Chopin have felt, when you denied the triple rhythm to a composition which is basically founded on that rhythm — and then consider his irritability!" "I did not intend to be unkind", said the great man. "I thought he wished it so!"

One of the things which particularly characterised Chopin's playing, was his 'rubato', in which the rhythm and time throughout remained accurate. "The left hand", he often said, "is the conductor. It must not waver, nor lose ground: do with the right hand what you will, and what you can". He told his pupils: "Supposing that a composition is to last a certain number of minutes. It may take just so long to perform the whole, but in details, deviations may occur". But the fine Russian pianist, Neilissov, told me a much better definition of Chopin's 'rubato', from Liszt. Liszt said to Neilissov in Weimar in 1871, "Do you see those trees? The wind plays in the leaves. Life unfolds and develops beneath them; but the tree remains the same. That is the Chopin 'rubato'".

In the variations and fluctuation of the tempo, Chopin was magnificent. Every single note was played with the highest degree of taste, in the noblest sense of the word. When he embellished — which he rarely did, it was a positive miracle of refinement. Chopin, by his very nature, was not fitted to interpret Beethoven or Weber, who paint along great lines, with great brushes. Chopin was a painter of pastels, but an unrivalled one! Contrasted with Liszt, he might well stand as an honourable equal with him — as his wife! The great B flat major Sonata of Beethoven (Op.106) and Chopin, are mutually exclusive.

About this time there lived in Paris a pianist by the name of Gutmann. He was a rough fellow at the piano, but of robust health, and herculean frame! Through these physical endowments, he impressed Chopin. He impressed George Sand, too, who extended to him her protection. Chopin praised Gutmann as the pianist whose interpretation of his works he most preferred. This was going far. He said he had "taught himself". This was really going too far — he, a giant! The Scherzo in C sharp minor, Op.39, is dedicated to him, and Chopin certainly had his prize-fighter in mind when he wrote it, for no left hand can take the chord in the bass in the sixth bar (D sharp, F sharp, B, D sharp and F sharp), least of all Chopin's hand, which arpeggioed over the easy-running, narrow-keyed Pleyel. Only Gutmann could 'knock a hole in the table' with that chord! I heard him at Chopin's. He played like a meat porter. So does Genius allow itself to be deluded when its own weaknesses sit in judgment. To the little Filtsch and me, Gutmann was a horror — we derided him. He learned absolutely nothing from Chopin, although Chopin took so much trouble to carve a tooth-pick out of this log! Nothing was ever heard of Gutmann — he was a discovery of Chopin's.

Chopin did not die of consumption. He died of a broken heart. He died at the same age as Mozart and Raphael. Liszt wrote a delightful book — it is called "Frédéric Chopin, by Franz Liszt" — a telling title. It was published by Escudier in Paris in 1845, and the entire edition was sold out, and I was unable to buy a copy in Berlin, Leipzig, or St. Petersburg. I had to read it in snatches, in the library of Count Wielhorski.

George Sand speaks of Chopin in her book "Un hiver en midi de l'Europe". It is a description of her stay in Majorca with Chopin, whom the Parisian doctors had sent to the Balearics when he was dangerously ill with consumption. She does not mention his name — she speaks of him only as l'Artiste. This is strangely secret! It is not depreciating, but for so great an artist, neither is it sufficiently appreciative. It is simply foolishly Parisian! How could a French nature understand Chopin? A Sand could never take a loftier flight in music than: "Frédéric, play me something!" or "Frédéric, a light!" L'Artiste was caught in a web, to which the spider was not lacking!

The compositions of Chopin opened a new era for the pianoforte. They run the risk, through lack of knowledge of the master's style of playing, of his intentions, of his views concerning the pianoforte, of remaining misunderstood. There is infinitely more in playing them than appears on the printed page. In expressing the inner soul of the instrument, and in their treatment of this, they rank higher than Weber. They go a step further. They maintain a supreme place in piano literature. They occupy a plane of ideas of a Novalis, or a Heine. They are the soul of the pianoforte — they cannot be "arranged" for any other instrument. They are less in touch with general ideas than with piano-ideas. They are great works in small frames — they are elegiac — lyric — on the standpoint of the composer's nationality. They are ideal, imperishable in the history of musical thought.

It is not my purpose to discuss the compositions of Chopin. It would be impossible to do so within the compass of these pages. A very much larger book would be necessary to give a complete picture of such great personalities as Liszt and Chopin, those "Dioscuri" of the modern pianoforte. Such a picture would, of necessity, include a complete historical view of art and literature as it was in the 1830's and 40's. The writers of that day were Balzac and Hugo, Dumas and Sue, Guizot and Villemain. The painters, Ary Scheffer and Delacroix; the composers, Rossini, Halévy, and Berlioz. They all belong to that historic view of civilization. Only in the focus of this light can the forms of Chopin and Liszt appear. In comparison with the later state of France — the total Napoleonic eclipse — the days of the Louis Philippe régime were a great epoch. "Notre voix avait un son éclatant qu'elle a perdu", Jules Janin wrote to me in 1853, when I was back in St. Petersburg. ("Our voice resounded in a way that has been lost".)

Musical literature is a concrete form of the activity of universal mental culture — a mirror of life amid whose conditions it had its origin.

The works of Chopin are no exception. Even Chopin was a son of his time, and only through the history of that time can he be understood. One can now make an absolute estimate of Bach, Haydn, Mozart and Beethoven, but not yet even of Weber.

Let us glance at the compositions of Chopin. So much in so little! Barely sixty-four authentic opus numbers, of which the "first steps" are a negligible quantity. And yet so much in the domain of the Mind.

What can one *not* say about the finished technique of Chopin? In this respect he ranks even higher than Weber. What can one say of his style of writing, his harmony, his modulation, his treatment of the piano in general, and the left hand in particular?

Chopin's tone-colour is like that of Raphael. He is the Raphael of the piano, though one must not seek his Madonnas in the churches — but in Life.

TAUSIG, CARL 1841–1871

III   Carl Tausig

Seldom has the death of an artist excited such universal sympathy as did that of Carl Tausig. He died, like Chopin, at the very height of his artistic career — in the strongest period of his musical development.

People who formed no part of the musical world, who had never heard Tausig play, but had heard only of him, honoured in Tausig not only the artist, but the man. In St. Petersburg, where Tausig had appeared but once, everyone spoke of the sad death in Leipzig as though it were one of their own near and dear ones who had died. How much more must this have been the case in Germany!

There was but one opinion of Tausig, even among the envious — for unfortunately there are such among us musicians, whether we scratch paper with pens, or play the piano, or scrape, or blow: only the thumper (tympani!) is harmless — and not even he, in Vienna, where he is a piano-virtuoso to boot!

There are some men who, upon their first appearance among us, make a lasting impression. To these few belonged Tausig.

In the Autumn of 1868 I was on my way to Europe's stronghold of Reason — Berlin — with the purpose of hearing Tausig. I was leaving behind me that charming butterfly-casket, Dresden, where one finds everything — as in the surgeon's case — except calibre.

I had had in Dresden such a variety of thoughts concerning the greatness of the composer of 'Der Freischütz' in the theatre, and at the piano, that I was too preoccupied in arranging them to take precautionary measures against the harvest wind blowing across the stubble, and I felt ill by the time we reached the lights which told me we were nearing Berlin. In contrast to the dimness of the Saxon nights, these lines of lamps appeared like an illumination in honour of some royal event. Berlin's 'calibre' had already begun to assert itself.

My artistic friend, the General-Intendant, Herr von Hülsen, had promised to give that evening — at my request — "Der Freischütz", from which I had not been separated for the past forty years. Knowing of my pedantic attention to the smallest detail in the performance of this work, he had given orders that my observations should be considered. He particularly asked: "We surely have not four trombones in Der Freischütz?" At Dresden, the introduction of the tuba in Weber's score struck me like a cuckoo's egg — quite anti-Weber in effect.

Herr von Hülsen had kindly offered me his box, and the fatality which attends a traveller brought me there long before the appointed time. I raised the green screen, and looked down into the orchestra, where but two people appeared in the semi-darkness, a viola and a clarinet. Said the viola to the clarinet; "Look sharp now. Draw back well in the dominant in the Overture, as we have been told. He is already here", pointing to my hiding place behind the screen. There was "calibre" for you!

Soon I was quite ill, and I was obliged to keep to my

room. I wrote to Tausig, whom I did not know personally, to say how much I regretted my inability to call upon him. In a few hours, a young man, somewhat under middle height, and delightfully unaffected, stood before me. "I am Carl Tausig. As you were unable to come to me, I have come to you — I shall come twice a day, if I can. You are of Liszt's household; so am I. We are comrades, and I am at your command whilst you are in Berlin". Chopin did not receive me thus in Paris! But this was Berlin, and not Paris. This was German cordiality, with no conventional iciness about it, and yet Tausig occupied the same position in Berlin as Chopin did in Paris. "Shall I send you a piano?" he said. "I have some very good ones".

Soon I was well enough to visit him, in the Taubenstrasse, where he then lived. The first time I went he was not at home, but I told the maid that I would wait for his return, and I made my way directly to the large bookcase in the first room. On the handsome bindings in the first row of books, I read the names of the greatest German philosophers. I was less astounded than pleasantly surprised. I had to wait quite a long time, so I examined one book after another, until I came to Arthur Schopenhauer, when Tausig laid his hand on my shoulder, saying: "Good books, are they not? They are my favourites, and they are not there for show. I read them often! Down here are my 'naturals'" — (he spoke jestingly of the natural histories) — "but your books are also here. Do you believe me? Here it is", and he drew it from the shelf. "Have you read them? Truly?" I said. He hesitated a moment, then looked me frankly in the eyes, and said: "I have read the French one; it made a fearful row at Liszt's".

"That is the poorest one", I replied. "You must read the German one. But only the last volume is for you —

the contemplation of the last works, for instance, the Op.101, A major Sonata. Holz and others in Vienna gave me some hitherto unknown particulars about it".

"The A major", said Tausig. "That is my favourite; that will be 'taken care of'. I will read it today". He took the book, and laid it on the table in the drawing-room.

We went into the next room, where the first piano presented itself. On it was an open copy of Beethoven's C sharp minor Sonata (quasi fantasia). "Did you know", I said, "that that should only be played in a room draped in black?"

"No, I did not know that at all".

"Holz wrote to me about it. He knows. Beethoven told him that he improvised the adagio while sitting beside the corpse of a friend in a room hung in black".

"That is lovely!" laughed Tausig, in his humorous manner. "If a pupil ever comes to torment me with it again, I shall say: "Is your room hung with black? If not don't play it"".

On my first visit to him, the piano played no part. In fact, I avoided it on purpose. Tausig said: "Well, we have always known each other, and you shall come every day. If you should hear a piano-racket when you come, that is the pupils! Escape into my study. There you will find the best piano, and plenty of scores. And newspapers, and the best cigars in Berlin. If you still hear the din, you must play against it; that is what I do, for other people give lessons at my house. I am collective, you see. But I can't stand it for too long. One more term and I'm off to the University to amuse myself with the study of philosophy and natural history, and to live, as far as possible, without a piano. Why not come along with me? What about Heidelberg? Berlin is too tiring — have you not noticed it? I am very fond of Berlin, but when I have had enough of this collective business, I shall pack my bags, and say 'enough'". That was characteristic of Tausig — how different from the brazen bonds of fashion in Paris.

At my second visit, Tausig played me the A major Sonata, Op.101. He played as I had never heard it played before! The first movement became an idyll; his handling of the finale with the fugue was a revelation. I said: "You divide the second theme in the finale — just before the fugue — between two instruments. I heard, so to speak, the oboe". This pleased him. "I am glad you noticed that", he said, "for that was my intention — only I have never told anyone". "The nuance in touch gives it away", I replied. "The first movement might be marked 'quasi chitarra'". "Two guitars, or four, if you like!" He played the movement so that I could hear the guitars. "But my legato is better", he said. "Let us keep to the grand style — Beethoven was no painter of miniatures. Now I will play you Chopin's A flat Polonaise. It is a little speciality of mine".

He played it, and I have never heard this triumphal, stupendously difficult piece played so perfectly, and with such easy mastery — or rather, with such complete obliviousness — of the technical difficulties. The Trio section, with the descending octaves in the left hand aroused an astonishment to which I gave unstinted expression. "This is beyond anything!" I cried. "How is it possible to play those octaves so evenly, so sonorously, and in that furious tempo? It goes from a murmuring pianissimo to a thunderous fortissimo!" "I told you it was a speciality! Look how small my hand is and I hold still closer together — my left hand is so formed that it runs by itself over the four notes, E, D sharp, C sharp and B. It is a natural phenomenon — I can do it for as long as you like, I won't get tired. That passage was written for me. Play those octaves with both hands, and you can't play them as loudly as I do!" I tried it. "There you are", he said, "Good, very good — but not so loud as mine. And after a couple of bars you will be tired, and so are the octaves. I don't think anybody else can play this passage like I do — and how few understand it! It is the tramp of the horses in the Polish Light Cavalry!" To me the supreme artistic moment was the exposition of the principal theme, at every entrance. It was the Poles, drunk with victory, sweeping away their beautiful partners in the dance. I said: "I have heard three scales played in my lifetime. First there was Liszt in the Scherzo of Beethoven's Op. 106 Sonata; then there was Henselt in Chopin's A minor Étude. And now you, in the A flat Polonaise. These are the Amazon streams of the piano — they overspread its entire extent; they are inimitable". Tausig replied: "No mortal can compete with Liszt. He dwells alone on a solitary height".

"Do you also play Weber?" I asked.

"I do not like to. I do not care to expose my inmost soul to the public, and that is what Weber demands, is it not? I play for the sake of Art, and when I satisfy Art, I satisfy mankind. However, I have played the 'Concertstück' many times, but it is not really within my province, like Beethoven's E flat Concerto, for example. That is my speciality — I shall play it at my début in St. Petersburg. The 'Philharmonics' have written to invite me — who are they? I shall play at their concert".

I told him: "The 'Philharmonics' as you call them, are a society, an old society, of St. Petersburg musicians who give two concerts a year in the Hall of the Nobles. They are for the benefit of widows and orphans". Tausig said: "I shall play at their concert — that is taken care of. I must see St. Petersburg. Do you yourself play much Beethoven?" "Not oftener than I go to church", I replied (and Tausig smiled at this), "which one does in moderation. One reads Beethoven, and will read him again and again. The real Beethoven lives in the orchestra".

"Coming back to Weber", said Tausig. "I have designs on the 'Invitation'. I wish to work on it, and I should like to talk with you about it. At my house we should be frequently disturbed. I can always find a free hour in the midst of my business, and if you have the time, there are suitable meeting places". I proposed the 'Maison Dorée' on 'Unter den Linden'. There we met and talked undisturbed. I admired the modesty of the great artist, and his eagerness to hear about Chopin, whom he had never had the opportunity to meet, and yet whose works he played so magnificently, as no one else could. I told Tausig of Chopin's peculiar treatment of the E flat Nocturne, Op.9. "That is interesting", said Tausig. "I will play through the bass with both hands myself; that is the place for the guitar — it shall be taken care of". But he was most interested in the fact that Chopin was so difficult and hard to please in the first four bars of the great C minor Nocturne (Op.48), apparently so simple. In the second bar occurs the semi-quaver figure D, E flat, F, G. The point was to glide from this G to C in the next bar. Chopin was never satisfied with this. He once said to me: "It is possible for you to do this, so you *must* do it". Eventually I did manage to satisfy him, but it took a long time. Sometimes the G was too short, and went to the C too quickly. Sometimes it was the other way round. "There is a meaning in it", said Chopin. It was just as difficult to please him with the lifting of the C before the quaver rest in the fourth bar. The C was always too short, or too long. I found a way out of this difficulty by drawing my finger along the key until I came to the end, and then drawing it off at the sharp corner. At last he was satisfied! But it was nothing, compared to the way in which Chopin himself played these two passages.

"I understand him perfectly", said Tausig, "and I shall take care of it". "Chopin intended the passage from G to C as a question; C gives the answer", I said. "That is just as I understand it", replied Tausig.

Just as rarely was Chopin satisfied with the very first bar of this Nocturne. The G and C in the treble should be prominent, since they are thematic. But they were always either too forte, or too piano. Chopin always used a Pleyel, an instrument with a light action, on which it is possible to do such shading more easily than on a mellower, fuller toned instrument. In the course of the next few days, Tausig played me both Nocturnes in a most finished manner — in fact, just as Chopin played them. He was pleased with himself, and said, "I should have known him!" Never was a composer so lovingly cherished by a virtuoso as was Chopin by Tausig.

One day Tausig appeared at my rooms early in the morning. "The Baroness Schweinitz invites you to a soirée at her house. She is my best pupil — indeed, I can scarcely call her a pupil. She is an Artist — and a very charming woman. You will meet interesting people there. The Baroness sends her excuses that the Baron has not called on you".

"I do not stand upon ceremony", I said, "and consider myself honoured by the invitation", I replied. "Then I will be here this evening at eight sharp, and we will drive to the Commandant's house together".

As we went through the vestibule into the large stuccoed hall, I said: "We have such halls in St. Petersburg, but not many". "I have often played here", said Tausig. "We give charity concerts here, in which the Baroness takes the lead". He walked to the side door of richly gilded mahogany, and threw it open. A suite of three salons, as bright as day, lay before us. We were most charmingly received by the Baroness in the first of these salons. Many distinguished artists belonging to the same musical circle of Tausig and the Baroness were there. There was Count Wimpffen, the Austrian Ambassador, and his wife; the Russian military plenipotentiary, Count Kutusov; and of course, the master of the house, Count Minister von Schweinitz. Tausig had not exaggerated — in a piece by Schumann, and a difficult brilliant piece of Tausig's, the Baroness proved herself to be a finished artist. Tausig's demeanour particularly pleased me; he quite effaced himself — it was as if he were not there at all, and yet he was everywhere, and the life of the animated conversation. This soirée will always remain one of my musical-social memories as one distinguished equally for intellectuality, and good taste. And since the death of the great artist who opened these doors for me, it has become a sacred one. In the higher circles of St. Petersburg, Berlin has a reputation for the formality of its etiquette. Yet here I was, in one of the best houses in Berlin opened to me, a stranger, whose only recommendation was that I was a friend of Tausig. As we drove home, Tausig said: "You gave me great pleasure. You sat at the piano just as *he* does!"

"You cannot believe that it ever occurred to me to imitate Liszt?" I was somewhat disconcerted. What could Tausig mean?

"You do not understand me. I am in earnest. There is no imitation about it — only an affinity in the spirit of the matter, understood by myself alone. It was not just the way you sat there, which is something you never even gave a thought to in your intercourse with the piano. It was *he* — as he lives and moves, I tell you. I could think only of *him* the whole evening!" Seldom is a master so lovingly worshipped as Liszt by Tausig! He had such a true, loyal, and loving heart! Such a sensitive nature should never have been wounded in its inner life. In Tausig's nature, humanism was predominant, like the artistic height on which he stood. Dark clouds gathered early over his life. The artist took refuge from them in his Art — his virtuosity was a veil behind which the artist sought to conceal the man. In his daily life he regarded as a simple duty what others call worshipping God. Not with any desire to shine, but with an earnest purpose, did Tausig take up the study of philosophy. He did not care for ostentation. Applause meant little to him, as, in fact, I had good opportunity to observe in St. Petersburg at his triumphs. He was dominated by a melancholy, a certain profundity of meditation, which often made him appear to be absent-minded when his thoughts were but too vivid. He tried to conceal the underlying vein of sadness, but it was clearly evident. The dash of humour in his conversation was but the flight of the spirit before the gloomy spectre. I discovered the key to his artistic nature in the manner in which he approached the 'Barcarole' of Chopin. "Do you know the 'Barcarole?' he asked me. "No", I replied. "Then I will play it to you on Sunday — but come early, before the hour of my friends, Davidson and C.F. Weitzmann, and some of the staff of the 'Kladderadatsch' usually drop in. This will be between ourselves; it is an interpretation which must not be attempted before more than two people. I will disclose myself to you — I love the 'Barcarole', but I seldom play it".

That same day I went along to a music store, and made a careful study of the work, with which I was unfamiliar. It did not please me at all. I thought it a long composition in nocturne style, bombastic in tonality, (F sharp major) and modulation — a tower of figuration built upon an insecure foundation! How sadly was I at fault!

Tausig explained the piece to me, which, as an exception, he did not play by heart. "This tells", he said, "of two persons; of a love scene in a secret gondola — we might even call it symbolic of lovers' meetings in general. That is expressed in the thirds and sixths. The dual character of two notes — or two persons — runs through the whole; it is all two voiced, or two souled. In the modulation into C sharp major (marked 'dolce sfogato'), you can recognise a kiss and an embrace — that is plain enough. When after three bars of introduction, this bass solo — an easy rocking theme — enters and this theme is nevertheless employed as an accompaniment throughout the entire work; on this lies the 'cantilena' in two voices, and we have a sweet dialogue. From the chain of double trills onwards, the story becomes difficult to tell — but that is my business. I'll take care of that. Turn the pages for me — and listen attentively!"

Seldom in my life have I heard so sweet, such a wonderfully beautiful story told at the piano. Every note spoke. The artist gave way to the man in Tausig, and how interesting both were!

How difficult, how impossible, except to subjective interpretation, it is to carry through nine pages of enervating music, in the same long-breathed rhythm (it is in twelve-eight) so much interest, so much emotion, so much drama, and so much action, that I regretted only that the long piece was not longer. Here, in the Barcarole, Tausig was the living impersonation of Chopin. He felt as he did, he played like him, he *was* Chopin at the piano!

I told him so frankly, and he felt the sincerity of conviction in my words. But he was always rather reserved — even suspicious — on such occasions, perhaps because he was never entirely able to dissipate his clouds!

Tausig gave concerts in Berlin entirely devoted to the works of Chopin. I believe that these were the first of such concerts, apart from the yearly 'concerts intimes' given in Paris by the master himself. How thankless undertakings of this sort usually are! How grateful we should be to Tausig for taking the initiative with regard to Chopin, whose pianistic importance is far too lightly estimated. Tausig also impressed me deeply with his interpretation of the F minor Ballade. It has, he told me, three requirements: "The comprehension of the programme as a whole — for Chopin writes according to programme, and to the situations in life best known to, and understood by, himself; the exposition of the motives in detail, and in an adequate manner; and the absolute conquest of the stupendous difficulties in the complicated passages and winding harmonies".

Tausig fulfilled all these requirements, presenting an embodiment of significance and the meaning of the work. The Ballade begins in the minor key of the dominant, and in the seventh bar comes to a stand before the 'fermata' on C major. The easy handling of these seven bars Tausig described thus: "The piece has not yet begun!" In his firmer, nobly expressive exposition of the principal theme, free from the sentimentality to which one might easily yield here, the "grand manner" found due scope.

It is an essential requirement of an instrumental virtuoso that he should understand how to breathe — and how to allow his hearers to take breath. By this, I mean a well-chosen incision — a lingering ("letting the air in", Tausig aptly calls it) — which in no way impairs rhythm and time, but rather brings them into stronger relief. It is a lingering which our signs of musical notation cannot adequately express. Rub the bloom from a peach or from a butterfly, and that which remains belongs only to the kitchen, or to natural history! It is the same with Chopin; the bloom consisted in Tausig's treatment of the Ballade.

He came to the first passage, as one would ordinarily call it; the motive from amongst the blossom and leaves, as one must say for Chopin — a figurated recurrence of the principal theme is in the inner parts — its polyphonic variant. A little thread connects this with the chorale-like introduction to the second theme. The theme is strongly and abruptly modulated, perhaps a little too much so. Tausig tied the little thread to a 'doppio movimento' in two-four time, thereby resulting in sextuplets, which threw the chorale into bolder relief. Then followed a passage 'a tempo'. in which the principal theme played a game of hide-and-seek! How clear all this became as Tausig played it. Of the technical difficulties he knew nothing — they simply did not exist. The most intricate, the most evasive parts were as easy as the most difficult — I might say easier! I admired the short trills in the left hand, which were trilled out quite clearly and independently, as if by a second player, and the gliding ease of the 'dolcissimo'. It swung itself into the higher register, where it came to a stop before A major, just as the introduction stopped before C major. Then, after the theme once more appeared, in a modified form (a variation), it comes under the pestle of a finely decorated coda, which demands the study of an artist, the strength of a robust player — in a word, the most vigorous pianistic health!

Tausig overcame this threatening group of terrifying difficulties whose appearance in the piece is well accounted for by the programme, without the slightest apparent effort. The coda, in its modulated harp tones, came to a stop before a 'fermata' which corresponded to those before mentioned, in order to cast anchor in the haven of the dominant, finishing with a witches' dance of triplets in double thirds. This eighteen page piece ends up with magnificent bravura.

Tausig's left hand was a second right — he never even appeared to notice difficulties. Anton Rubinstein called him "the infallible". Liszt described his fingerrs as "brazen", and Sérow said to me, whenever we spoke of pianists, "Hear Tausig; you *must* hear Tausig!" His most distinguishing characteristic was that he never played simply for effect, but was always completely absorbed in the piece itself, and its artistic interpretation. The general public never quite understood this objectivity. Whenever serpents are strangled, it wants to know just how big and how dangerous they are, and judge this by the performer's behaviour. The general public, in fact, thinks that whatever looks as if it is easily accomplished, is not really difficult at all, and that the son or daughter at home might do it equally well! But it was this outward calm, this perfect steadiness of Tausig's attitude, which crowned his virtuosity.

Well might he say — as I heard him once remark — "I am no drawing-room pianist, it is only in public that I can command all my resources". Playing with eccentric gestures, with all one's limbs may be, and indeed is, very effective with the public. But such elements are inimical to art. Tausig's playing was flawlessly moulded. How he would have charmed Chopin, whose perfect ease and grace in overcoming the greatest technical difficulties he possessed, together with far superior strength and power.

Before I left Berlin I discussed with Tausig Liszt's 'Don Juan' Fantasia, which is a work demanding the highest degree of virtuoso playing. Tausig said, with noble modesty: "For a long time I could not conquer this piece. Not until I returned to Bach, and the last Beethoven Sonatas, and studied them again and again, would it surrender itself to me. You raise no objection to my interpretation of the 'Don Juan' Fantasia? Well, I can tell you that I tell myself I have not conquered the difficulties — I have only attacked them. Liszt alone is superior to them — only he! That is the secret of the impression he makes. You said in your French book: 'He is the Paganini of the piano'. That is true, and it pleased him, but it says far too little. Liszt possesses an absolute mastery over the entire realm of musical art; he is a predestined composer in the largest forms. Out of his great diversity of talents, arises his virtuosity. Paganini never soared so high as Liszt — he stopped at virtuosity!"

In fact, Liszt's technique has been thought of as a spiritualised technique— as a new train of ideas, as a thread spun from Bach and Beethoven to us, reaching to the compositions of Liszt, as to the latest expression of the possibilities of the piano. The great piano-virtuosos of the century may be compared with continents and countries. Liszt, Chopin, and Henselt are continents. Tausig, Rubinstein, and Bülow are countries.

Thalberg was only the correct "gentleman-rider" of the piano during the past forty years, which seems to lie a whole century behind us. A rider, no matter how well he sits upon his horse, has to get off sometimes. But not Thalberg. He rode perpetually. He called it "Fantasie" — like the one on Moses, for example. He made music like a trumpeter in the Kaufmann Museum in Dresden — blown through the air, but not through the soul. Thalberg was the well-groomed piano — but who saddles a note of his nowadays? Only one of his lubrications has musical promise, and that only in the beginning (his opening trot). That is his second Caprice (in E flat major) in which the principal motive is charmingly bridled, and at the end of the interminable 'performance', as the English call musical productions, sets off at a veritable steeplechase and clears the fence in a succession of leaps of two octaves! Thalberg once said that he would undertake to play side by side with Liszt, but that Liszt must sit behind a screen, and must not be seen whilst he is at it! There, and for the first time, Thalberg would have been thrown, for the soul of Liszt could stay behind no screen! "You resemble the spirit which you comprehend, not me!" Liszt might have told him.

Thalberg was a finished man-of-the-world at the piano. The thumb of his right hand was his groom, whom he had promoted to the exalted position of Conductor of the Melody! The shifting of the accompaniment to the middle range of the piano was not the invention of Thalberg. It was introduced by Beethoven in the 'Largo' of his first Piano Concerto (C major) which appeared in 1801; then again by Weber in the 'Andante' of his D minor Sonata, and in his 'Invitation'. and in the Rondo of his E flat major Concerto.

It is often said that the piano reached its climax in Liszt and Chopin. Every period has its 'raison d'être'. Virtuosity had hers, and Tausig is the best evidence of this fact. It is the same in creative work. If Life were divided between Church and Theatre — between the things symbolized by these factors — their representatives on the piano would be, first and foremost Beethoven and Weber.

Weber's sympathy was with life in general, whilst Chopin's with the life of the higher classes of society in particular. Chopin did not feel less deeply than Weber because he *felt* in Paris. But Chopin's sympathy was special, and Weber's was general — he sprang from German soil! There is no trace of opera or symphony in Chopin's music, while Weber's piano music is haunted by these elements, like the fantastic will-o'-the-wisps in the Wolfsschlucht. Chopin is always pure pianoforte, with a masterly pianistic treatment and style of the instrument far superior to that of Weber. Chopin commands all technical resources of the piano, which Weber never mastered to such a degree.

The relationship of Chopin to Beethoven and Weber on the piano, is that of a peer to these great men. Beethoven's piano music might well be regarded as 'sketches' for orchestra and quartets, in the same way that Kaulbach's sketches in the cathedral in Berlin are to be understood as paintings. Beethoven, as the Genius incarnate of the symphony, is always symphonic in all that he writes; especially so in his piano concertos and the violin concerto. His thoughts, in their flight, leave the piano, never to return — they are lost in the infinitude of the Idea! Even his quartets are abbreviated symphonies, in spite of their quartet-like idiom.

Tausig understood how to discriminate in Beethoven as well as in Weber. He played Beethoven's A major Sonata (Op.101) with the most charming piano-colouring; the powerful orchestral Fantasia in the F minor Sonata (Op.57) — called the "Appassionata" (as though all his sonatas were not "Appassionata") he performed orchestrally. He played the A flat major Sonata (Op.110) with Pompeian colouring, and the last Sonata, (Op.111), was colossal!

Nothing is more important to the virtuoso than a profound understanding of the tone-poet whom he undertakes to interpret. In this, Tausig's lofty general education stood him in good stead, together with his fine taste which was largely the result of scientific research in all things. Whatever one might say, as an authoritative musical critic, Tausig takes an exceptional position, although, of course, our great master, Liszt, will for all time be taken as the highest standard of musical criticism.

Before I speak of my meeting with Carl Tausig in St. Petersburg, I must relate one more reminiscence of Berlin, of that late Autumn of 1868, ever to be remembered for the artist's genial kindliness.

Once, when we were quite alone, Tausig made me sit at his piano, and said: "Play the highest part of this — this piece cannot be known to you". It was a set of short, expressive compositions for four hands by Schumann. "There", he said, when I had finished. "You play that exactly as *he* would!" I looked up at him, confused. On the one hand, I could not think that he was teasing me, and on the other hand it had not seemed to me that I had played so well. "I am in earnest", he repeated, "You played it just as *he* would!" "But there is not much to play", I said, "only to understand". "That is just it — you can't teach that to your lady pupils! It quite astonished me — I could hear your journeys — your foot-tours in Switzerland". At this time, Tausig could still be humorous. When I saw him two years later (1870) in St. Petersburg, this part of his character had quite disappeared. A few days after my 'sight-reading test' I went to Tausig with two books in my hands. "Ah", said he, "now you are going to take revenge for your examination. I wished to see — never mind. Tell me in what *I* am going to be examined". "Here you are". I said placing the books in front of him. "Sonatas progressives et agréables". Tausig laughed most heartily. "And what is that to us?" "To give pleasure", I replied. "These are little operas in disguise, by Weber. Just play the bass part, and listen attentively. The original is for piano and violin. Cranz, the Hamburg publishers, told me that this arrangement is by Czerny. Sonata No. 1 in F major — really a Sonatina. Allegro — Before the gate, Whitsuntide. Larghetto; Grandmother's story at the Fireplace, B major. Rondo — 'amabile', F major, The Posthorn! There is nothing of all this in the music, but listen, and I will bring it out", I said confidently. "Very well, then", said Tausig. "Let us begin at the fireplace . . . yes, that is really interesting . . . once more! You play it very well". "Twenty years of faithful wedlock", I told him. "What!" he replied, "And still in love! Well, let us go before the gate . . . Also very interesting. But the 'Amabile' — the Posthorn story — is nothing . . . But the eight bar 'minore' . . . that is by a master, again . . ."

"Sonata No. 2", I showed him. "Moderato, guitar — a German in Seville, G major. Adagio in C minor — From a Lost Opera, Didome abbandonata. Rondo, G major — Polish Air, In the Country, St. John's Day".

Tausig remarked: "This Spain might be in Germany".

"Just like the Spain in 'Don Giovanni'."

"You think so . . . Well perhaps! Adagio, interesting. Rondo, charming. Modulation to B flat, to the lower dominant (C major), delicious . . . let us play it again . . . Oho, how abruptly the thing ends!"

"Sonata 3. Air russe, D minor, The Truth about Russia, Unknown in Germany". (How ingenuously Tausig glanced at me!). "Maggiore, charming. I have written above it 'amoroso.' Rondo, presto, D major — Dance of the Elves, utterly charming — beyond description!" "Let us have the Elves then", urged Tausig. "That is a serious matter", said Tausig. "The Rondo is very beautiful, and how abrupt at the close. That must be true! Now the Rondo over again", he commanded. "Notice the festoons of flowers from the thirteenth bar", I said. "Another seduction of Giovanni — but I must beg you to play the 'primo' now, because I do the scales so badly". "There is one in the bass which is more important — the whole orchestra enters there. I shall stay below!" answered Tausig. We played the Rondo three times. It is not long — only eighty-four bars in all — but how much there is in it! "A proper country residence — without mortgage, and with elves! Let us play through the rest at once".

"Sonata 4 in E flat major, Sunday, Game of Skittles. Sunflowers by the Bowling-alley. What fine honest folk these are we shall find out from the ninth bar onwards. Rondo, vivace, modestly illuminated garden".

Tausig broke in: "But wait! How charmingly he accents the 'beloved brethren' motive".

"Sonata 5 — In the Theatre, in A major. Andante con moto, theme from the opera Sylvana, four-four. Do you know it? Weber must have loved this theme — he worked it into variations for solo clarinet accompanied by almost solo piano. That set is Op.33 in B major. This set in A is Op.10. Which do you think is the earlier work?"

"That is where doctors disagree", quoted Tausig aptly. "According to all good methodology, the completer work is the last, I think."

"Yes, but in our Op.10 we have this devilish march-variation, Marcia Maestoso. Only the most finished master could have written that! The Finale Siciliano is charming, too".

Tausig: "That No. 5 is altogether too pretty! Do you know, I have an idea. One could arrange these things as a Weber Fantasia, for drawing-room purposes. I shall do it one day". (An idea which should be taken up some time — one *must* love Weber; Rubinstein loved him).

"The 6th Sonata is insignificant and the closing Polonaise is weak — although there is a pretty violoncello solo or would you call it bassoon?" Tausig: "I would call it a cornet à pistons!" So 'scherzoso' was he in those days!

And so we passed every day — unfortunately for only six weeks.

Two years passed. The news that Tausig was coming before Easter for a concert season, aroused the musical contingent of St. Petersburg. It was in March, 1870. I went immediately to Tausig, as soon as he arrived. He was staying at the Hotel Demuth. He greeted me kindly, but I could see that he was a changed man. There was a cloud on his features; he was no longer cheerful.

"You must forgive me" he said tactfully, "that I did not go to see you, but I make no visits now. I leave the hotel only to go to my concerts, and then not until the very last minute, when everything is quite ready, so that I can seat myself at the piano the moment I arrive". He handed me a cigar. "These, at any rate, are the same", he said, with a sad smile. I talked to him of unimportant matters — it seemed the best course to pursue, although I was not yet certain of the reason. He must have thought so too, as he rose quickly, and said: "I must play you your 'Invitation'". But he only played the passage which, in his arrangement of the piece he has added a 'moto contrario' for the left hand. I was quite astonished at this virtuosity soaring freely, as it were, into space, even in a domain where I felt so thoroughly at home. "If it amuses you", he said, "I will do it again. I can play it even faster!" This time he played the passage pianissimo in a fabulous prestissimo tempo, smiled, and rose.

The delivery was not natural; it was 'scurrilous', as Master Hoffmann (Kreissler) was wont to say. The artist must have been grieving! At my request, however, he played through the entire piece, together with his

81

arabesques, which were a speciality of his arrangement. The 'Invitation', one of the most well-known pieces in the entire piano repertoire, was written by Weber some fifty years ago, yet here it was, young and fresh. I think it is the most significant and most gratifying piece in rondo form without accompaniment, that we possess. This tender, yet remarkably brilliant inspiration, is intended to be an intimate piano piece, and finds its natural place in the family circle, and in the drawing-room. If it is to appear before an audience of two thousand, it must, of course, put on its ball-attire, and appear in the full panoply of the modern, Olympian concert grand, an instrument reaching far beyond the possibilities of the piano known to Weber. Thus Tausig treated the 'Aufforderung' in his variation. The rocking 'cantilena', to which, in the original, the accompaniment is in the middle register of the piano, was placed by Tausig as a bass voice — the voice appropriate to a dancer declaring his love to his partner — whereas in Weber's arrangement this charming 'cantilena' is more representative of the whole scene.

To me, the most artistic part of Tausig's interpretation of the 'Aufforderung' was the 'minore', which, when he played it, was given an almost boisterous effect. I told him so. His reply was: "It is pleasant that you should praise my reading throughout, when all your life you have played it differently! Will you be writing about it?" "Certainly I will", I replied. "I shall write all about your arabesques, and I shall say just what I told you. Personally, and for the best reasons, I shall continue to follow Weber's text!" He laughed, for once, in his old manner. "Yes", he said, "it is devilish hard! See, here, where the 'motus contrarius' touches the minor, and yet the polished floor of the ballroom must remain as smooth and mirror-like as ever! I have often thought of you when I played it. But I shall play it much better this evening — my wings grow when I play in public. You will see tonight. But now, goodbye — and, like a good fellow, don't come here again, for I have become an unbearable companion!" There was a touch of his old Berlin humour!

I always like to go early to concerts and operas on special occasions. I like to see the tribe of double-basses stretch out their long necks; to see the wind-players fumble in their cases; to see the trumpets and kettle-drums making ready, and the violins in conference. What thoughts arise! There is something positively grand about an orchestra. It is the very summit, from where everything proceeds, and to where everything returns; that is the cosmic idea, and the orchestra is the Church of Instrumentalism. Such an important fraction of civilization should never be invited to an improvised meal, but only to a symposium!

This time Beethoven's E flat major Concerto was on the programme — a worthy banquet! The fate that compels the traveller (and in large cities one always travels) brought me there one hour before the time the concert was due to begin. The vast interior of the Hall of the Nobles in St. Petersburg usually resembles a dimly lit crypt at such times. Although the hall itself was only half lit, since it was so early, it was already completely full! I had not seen such a sight for forty years. I hastened to the artist's room so that I could tell Tausig all about it. He was not there, however. He appeared at each concert now just in time to play.

This hall has, for the past forty years, been the official meeting place of the nobility, and it is one of the most beautiful — if not the most beautiful hall in Europe. The roof is supported on either side by twelve Corinthian columns of polished white stucco, in two stories (with a gallery). There were three pillared doorways at each end, through which one descends a few steps into the hall. Between the pillars hang twenty-eight magnificent chandeliers, and from the ceiling hang eight more of colossal size. In such surroundings, the accoustics, it must be admitted, leave something to be desired; but nevertheless, they are good. The hall is often used for festivals, balls, and court ceremonies. The orchestra platform is built out into the hall.

With this orchestra, and in this hall, have appeared all the greatest musicians of Europe. Here played Franz Liszt! Here came the great singers, Pasta, Viardot, Sontag (Countess Rossi). Here played the violinists, Vieuxtemps, Ernst, Sivori, Ole Bull. Here sang the great Rubini. In fact, here took place all the grand functions of the musical life of St. Petersburg. The two Counts Wielhorski were the leaders in taste — not by force, but by their artistic superiority, and hence with more enduring result. These two patrons and artists, unique in the musical annals of Europe, never occupied an official position in music. Their followers were drawn to them organically — by natural selection, as it were. Rubinstein, who belonged to this great musical period, once said to me; "In these days, everything is public".

"Dat vincla libertas", said I to myself. (Freedom brings shackles.)

At Tausig's concerts, every seat in this great hall was taken — even the balcony facing the Emperor's box which belongs to the diplomatic corps, was given up to the public. The gallery was a compact mass of men and women, whilst in the entrances, between the windows and the pillars, stood row upon row of closely packed people, the last row even standing upon the window ledges!

Thus was Tausig received! In keeping with the artist's modest manner of presenting himself, the entrance prices were also modest, although they were high by German standards. They ranged from one rouble for a seat in the gallery, to as high as two, three, and five roubles for the reserved seats. By the morning of the first concert, Tausig's agent had already sold more than three thousand roubles' worth of tickets. The gross proceeds amounted to twice that sum, and all three of his concerts were equally well attended. It was the same story in Moscow, where all the tickets were sold even before Tausig arrived! Yet, in spite of this, when he returned from Moscow to St. Petersburg, he would not be persuaded to give one more concert.

Well, Tausig appeared upon the platform, and seated himself at the piano, which he had brought with him from Berlin. He was greeted with a storm of applause such as an artist returning home after a long absence might hardly hope to receive.

Now the E flat major Concerto struck up!

The artist seemed to be completely oblivious of himself — I saw instantly — that he might fully recognise the sway of his imperial mistress, Art, in one of her noblest works.

His club-strokes, meeting the onset of the orchestra, were fearful! These were his answers to the rigours of life, as they affect the artistic soul! Tausig played the concerto by heart, as he played all his programmes. He was a rhapsodist, drunk with the passion of the immortal poet. The most difficult passages were like toys in his hands! I never heard a more fiery, a more masculine exposition of the flame of the Rondo.

And how uniquely this Rondo rushed into the hall! In the delicate second theme, Tausig seemed to be saying: "It is nothing to me now — all is over!" In the leaps in C (in the modulation) which were like sparks of electric, he said: "This is I!" It was the very epitome of delicacy, the most perfect elegance. I remembered then what he had told me in Berlin: "That concerto is my speciality!"

I cannot improve upon what the 'Kölnische Zeitung', 1871, said of this concerto: "This concerto is a truly noble tone-poem. All it requires, in order to appear in the full splendour of its steel panoply, is a knightly player — not one who would strip off its armour and take away its weapons, to bring it forth clothed in a silken jacket and shoes!" Tausig was this knightly player in St. Petersburg.

His solo playing in St. Petersburg extended over the entire repertoire, from Bach and Scarlatti to Mozart and Beethoven; from Field to Chopin; from Weber and Schumann to Liszt. All styles were simple to him. He united in himself the characteristics of the most diverse natures!

Let us sum up the attributes of this great artist now torn from our midst. His command of all musical resources was so great, that in this command resided the poetry of a conqueror holding sovereign sway over material and machinery — a poetry peculiar and apart. His talent for the strict style (fugue, the imitative style) was unique. He played fugues, and indeed, all contrapuntal music, with the charm of the most charming treatment of the freer styles. It was once said of him that the neatness with which he brought out every part, and the nuances of his touch, made this academic style popular, generally intelligible, universally interesting. In the fugue we confront the *letter*, into which we have to breathe the *spirit* of Art, not a subjective personality; an artistic subjectivity in a narrow sense. Tausig possessed, in a high degree, the power of subordinating his own nature to the necessity of his art, so that in the playing of fugues he was peculiarly at home. He was the possessor of the entire range of the utmost possibilities of the piano as expressed in the compositions of Liszt, and he was a magnificent interpreter of Chopin.

In a word, he was one of the most prominent virtuosos the world has ever known, an "infaillibler triumphator" at the piano.

'Have, anima pia! Te! amicissimum sodalem — moriturus salutat!'

HENSELT, ADOLF. 1814–1889

IV   Adolf Henselt

Arthur Schopenhauer, who apprehends the world, in his philosophy, as Will and Idea, once said: "The greatest good fortune is never to have been born". Never to have written may also be regarded as a fairly acceptable piece of good fortune! The difficulty about writing is that you must not only talk — you must say something. By writing, you always make more enemies than friends, and your gain is but a symbol. In the 'Berliner Musikzeitung' Nos. 37–39, 1868, appeared a series of articles comprising Liszt, Chopin, and Tausig, and holding out a promise of a continuation, more especially because a halt was made before the most unique phenomenon of this century on the keyboard — Adolph Henselt. If we speak of Henselt as the most unique phenomenon on the keyboard, we now have to justify this designation by means of personal evidence.

In absolute power over every possible resource of the piano, and therefore over every style, Liszt is understood to be *cosmic* — supreme. Tausig, who treated the apparatus, the medium, as an art in itself, leaned thereby more towards universality, than individuality. Chopin was too individual in production to be able to express his entire individuality in reproduction, as an artist deficient in physical command of the medium. We say his *entire* individuality; for in details of interpretation, in a natural elegance all his own — springing from true feeling, and not from artificial effect — in taste and fervency of all his conceptions, the pianist Chopin likewise discovered incomparable individuality of its kind — a Polish individuality with French breeding, and French manners, with the advantages and disadvantages of both nationalities.

Because of his lack of physical power, Chopin composed everything in song style. Every detail of his work conforms to this style — in this art he was a pastel-painter such as had never before existed. His Mazurkas are the journal of his spiritual journeys into the socio-political domain of his Polish dream-world! There his powers of reproduction were at home; there dwelt the individuality of Chopin the pianist. He represented his dreamland, Poland, in the salons of Paris, and even dared, in the reign of Louis Philippe, to predict political independence for his beloved country. Chopin was the only *political* pianist. He interpreted Poland; he composed Poland!

French life, and the French schools of Art and Science in general, were not altogether without influence on Franz Liszt. This was shown at the time by the fact that this great *apparition* at the pianoforte, the greatest phenomenon ever known on the pianoforte — that Liszt placed in the front rank the attainments of a mechanical skill not entirely free from a certain stereotyped formalism — French precision acting upon conventional lines — and brought its influence to bear on conventionalism and on all things "that Fashion sternly parts", as Schiller has it.

His style at that time, was sufficient unto itself, just as the French language is self-sufficient. The artist's genius — "his spark of immortality" — freed him from

French influences, and drew him ever closer to Germany, the collective fatherland of musical art — an advantage which obtained for him mastery over all other styles. By means of German intellect, from German depth, and with German knowledge and power, he entered at will into the soul-life of France and Italy.

Midway between Liszt and Chopin — one might say the connecting link between their contrasting natures — stands Henselt, a primitive German phenomenon, a 'Germania' at the pianoforte. Henselt is German in everything, in production and in reproduction.

For the past thirty-two years Henselt has lived in St. Petersburg, where he never appears in public. Twice every year he visits Germany, but even there he is heard only by a chosen few. One might say that Henselt is the only artist among the great pianists who is Liszt's equal — although in the specifically subjective domain he belongs to a more specialized sphere. Henselt alone has, first of all, the same command over the resources, in fullness of tone, and the same finish of execution; this perfection of execution is unapproachable — beyond all comparison. However, we do not care for comparisons, but will examine each of these phenomena separately, upon its own ground.

In his creation, in his manner, in his whole personality Henselt is German — thoroughly German, without general polish. He has his own peculiar polish, his own peculiar finish. He is a law unto himself. By this law he departs from the good old school, and arrives at some very individual results. He was once a pupil of Hummel — that is, if one can speak of him as being anyone's *pupil*! However, one must begin somewhere, and therefore it is necessary to mention that the foundation of Henselt's technique is a very solid one. We should call it 'classic' had the term not been so stupidly misused, and were it not odious to us. We shall rather call Henselt's mode of expression, taken as a whole, romantic — in feeling and spirit like Weber, whom he much resembles in disposition. Romanticism is a distinctly German characteristic which is most prominently developed in Henselt. Even when the artist develops a lighter vein, and offers a modest drawing-room piece, the ordinary listener discerns sentimentality — albeit refined sentimentality. There too, in the smallest possible compass, is Henselt romantic in the same way that Weber is romantic in 'Freischütz' where even Annchen's simple songs are flooded with moonlight for every one that has taste to appreciate them.

In his outward appearance, Henselt is also specifically German. In his dignified, simple carriage, in his self-poised manner combined with the sincerest modesty, he never is or will be satisfied with his achievement — a fact which the keen observer easily recognizes, and only the vulgar misjudges. Henselt pursues an ideal of perfection, which never permits him a moment of unalloyed delight. Hence it is that Henselt is the only artist to exhibit the phenomenon — remarkable, indeed, but founded in his innermost nature — that immediately on finishing playing a given piece or movement, he will, to the utmost astonishment and delight of his chosen audience, play it over, and even over again, as though inspired to do so at the command of some higher power — so unconscious is he of his surroundings! These were moments of supreme ecstasy, of entire isolation from the outside world — moments in which a man is no longer master of himself, moments when the artistic soul alone is active. These were moments when the artist approaches nearer to his ideal, which he longs with such passionate yearning to reach the outer world, that is his own self, and the impression made upon his audience is quite forgotten! At these moments, had Henselt any suspicions that there was an audience, he would gladly have had them thrown out of the window! Such is the results of my observations of Henselt during the past thirty-two years!

One does not experience mere enjoyment in hearing Henselt, one is intoxicated and elevated at the same time. Another distinctive characteristic in Henselt is that in the very midst of a composition, wherever his enthusiasm seizes him, whenever he soars towards his ideal, he reinforces the singing melody that fills his heart, by humming it himself! The artist's voice is anything but lovely, and ruins the effect, as he knows full well when he is told that he has been singing again, for he himself does not know it. Never, never have I heard such a magical 'cantilena' flow from the pianoforte, as in those moments when Henselt's voice joins his playing. But even then he is never satisfied. He is never happy for a moment.

Henselt first appeared in St. Petersburg in the concert season of 1838, and since that time has seldom been away from the city. I happened to be at Count Wielhorski's when Henselt first called there. I shall never forget the extraordinary impression he made when he played his F sharp major Étude, "Si j'etais oiseau." It was like an Aeolian harp hidden beneath garlands of the sweetest flowers! An intoxicating perfume was crushed from the blossoms under his hands — soft, like falling rose-leaves, the alternating sixths, which in one and the same octave, pursued, teased, embraced, and enraptured! Such a charming rich fullness of tone in his 'pianissimo' had never before been heard on the piano! After this most delicate whisper in the principal theme, the 'minore' entered energetically, gathering force from one degree to the next, and taking the instrument by storm — only to lose itself in a magic dialogue in sixths! Thirty-two years have passed since that performance, but the enchanting picture still lives fresh in the memory.

Henselt must have realised how enchanted we were with his performance, for as soon as he finished the piece, he started again at the most touching part of his poem, and played it through a second time, with quite different gradations of tone and expression. It was like gleaning after a harvest of joy. He must have been well pleased with himself when he read his instant triumph in the eyes of connoisseurs of such high standing as the Counts Wielhorski.

In quite a different style, flowing more quietly, broadly, and deeply, he went on to play his 'Poëme d'amour' in B major, which passing over from an unquestionably new nocturne style, changes to a not less deeply felt *allegro* in variation form, and closes with the highest degree of bravura in arpeggios covering the whole extent of the instrument — and which he hurled like heavy well-aimed spears — although never exceeding the limits of euphony, or once over-stepping the measure of power allowed to the pianoforte.

Such playing had never before been heard. Such tenderness, and such force, and a depth of meaning so sufficient to itself, with all its euphemistic concessions to the audience, made it an artistic feat — a phenomenon wholly unique.

The great success of the concert which he gave at the big theatre was so extraordinary, the result so great, towering above everything of the kind which had been known abroad, the victory over the old school so indisputable — that the artist acceded to the outspoken wishes of the public, and took up residence in St. Petersburg. Henselt's coming to us marked the obsolescence of the Hummel-Field school of piano playing, and brought the piano into quite a different channel. A deep shadow fell over the old literature, which was represented in St. Petersburg by Charles Mayer, who in his way was a finished, nimble-fingered, smooth, but very dry pianist, and by Reinhardt, who had been a pupil of Field in Moscow, but who resembled him only in the superficial part of piano ornamentation, and not in the spirit of his interpretations. Mayer himself swore by Field, and claimed to be his best pupil; but both these musicians understood little of Beethoven, and nothing at all of Weber. Mayer had the presumption to transfer his loyalties to Hummel, whose compositions, in the twenties and thirties, passed for the highest kind of piano music. Now for Henselt, Hummel was but a starting point. With Henselt's compositions, aside from their unparalleled interpretation by the composer, a new era began: the era of lyric personality, subjective dramatic intention, a freedom in execution, bearing internal evidence of a real human right to be. This tendency, this new salon-music, had its origin in the good old school, and belonged, from a technical standpoint, to a sound tradition. But now it had nothing more to do with schools and pedants, with pattern and routine. Henselt's compositions seek to express emotion, and not speculative musical ideas. They cannot be judged merely by reading them — they must be played, or heard.

The abstract idea, so powerful, for example, in Schumann, is foreign to Henselt. Nowhere in his compositions do we find the voids which in Hummel are hidden behind interminable tinklings. Henselt paints pictures of deep feeling within small frames, and his mastery of the medium enables him — through polyphony, positions, extensions, generally to make the most of every technical possibility of the instrument, to give interest to compositions in which the original idea was of slight value. It is the most fruitful treatment of the piano, beyond which Liszt and Chopin were able to pass only in details, not essentials.

Time is generally the most righteous judge of worth. Henselt's compositions have held their own in the piano repertory for forty years. That is saying a great deal — that is a proof that they embody living thought which must survive fashion and the influence of the moment — that they are, in fact, vital thoughts, which cannot be said of any of their contemporaries. It is not merely the fundamental expression of love-yearning, together with a strong dash of romanticism, in Henselt's compositions, but also their tragi-dramatic aim, which give them value and importance. In the Études 'Eroica' and 'Dankgebet nach Sturm' there is an amount of energy, sincerity, and dramatic effect which, before his time was not to be found on the piano. Henselt is, altogether, a phenomenon, unsurpassed by any other of our day, which in its place and period, is of equal rank with Liszt — that is, overmastering epoch-making in art. Henselt is no music-spirit pure and simple — he belongs essentially to the piano, and is indissolubly bound to it. Hence it is that Weber and Henselt are so much alike in spirit — that Weber is much more sympathetic to the artist than Beethoven. Weber lives in the region of loving human souls, whereas Beethoven's influence over the world is through the strength and power of speculative thought! These two aims are not opposed, they run parallel. They do not interfere with one another; they divided the world between them. Of Beethoven's first three piano trios (Op.1), Henselt said, in his pithy way: "They grew; the later ones were made". He thought the same, in a higher degree, of Beethoven's piano sonatas, which, as everybody, knows, form a cult by themselves.

I know that I lay myself open to contradiction here — it might be war to the knife, but for the fact that I shall never venture to argue with Henselt! His obstinacy and tenacity are too strong — *he* would never yield! He sits walled in by his own convictions, walled in with the precepts of his good old school, even though these precepts are no longer impregnable. But one example is worth mentioning. Beethoven in the finale of the choral symphony, uses the chord of the seventh on F, in D minor, together with the minor ninth and the full dominant harmony, so that the entire diatonic minor scale of D is heard at once. At a dinner in St. Petersburg, which Henselt gave in honour of Berlioz, the latter referred to this chord as a "monster", which he could not understand. Henselt rose from the table, opened a piano, and seated himself — not without some irritation — on the keys, and said: "It sounds something like this!"

Henselt says that Bach can never grow old, and this is very true. But the reason for this lies in the nature of the fugue as a conventional form, and not in the superiority of the thought. Such a study of Bach as Henselt made, every day of his life, has never before been heard of! He played the fugues most diligently on a piano so muffled with feather quills that the only sound heard was the dry beat of the hammers against the muffled strings; it was like the bones of a skeleton rattled by the wind. In this manner the artist spared both his ears and his nerves, for he reads, at the same time, on the music-rack, a very thick, good book — the Bible — surely the most appropriate companion for Bach. After he had played Bach and the Bible quite through, he begins all over again. The few friends whom Henselt allows to approach him in those late hallowed evening hours, he requests to continue their conversation — that does not disturb him in the least. But the rattle of the skeleton in the piano disturbs *them*, and tortures their nerves instead of quieting them. Thus seated at a dumb piano with Bach and the Bible for company, the composer of so many love-songs, of the 'Poëme d'amour', the most keen-eared tone-reveller among the virtuosi, earned his daily artistic bread! One might meditate much on this; it is a long leap — a 'salto mortale' — from the Prophets to Theocritus and Tibullus!

Such a strange phenomenon is this artist. One might add that he is, so to speak, a second Faust-Wagner: "In truth I know much, but I would know all".

The effect Henselt produced in St. Petersburg was so great, that he became all at once the all-absorbing topic of conversation at the pianoforte. He concentrated, in his own person, the function of instructor in all the most influential circles and at Court, where he was immediately appointed Court Pianist, by the Empress. He kept open house, gave no more concerts, and devoted his entire energy to composition and teaching — his lessons he managed with almost unheard of punctuality and energy. His Piano Concerto in F minor dates from this time — also his Trio in A minor, which by reason of the contemporary movement, stands in the constellation of Mendelssohn.

In order to hear Henselt, one had either to become a pupil, which was not easy, or to belong to his circle of intimate acquaintances, which was still more difficult. To the latter, he played on Sunday mornings in Winter for several hours — occasions of the most solemn gatherings of the faithful. These 'matinées' at Henselt's, as they were called, were most extraordinary. The artist would play one piece after another, without halt or rest, often without interruption. He thought little about his audience — unless the foremost beauties of the city happened to be present. He appeared to regard performances as in the light of exercises of a loftier nature, for he was always playing exercises. For years he always had a dumb piano on his knees, on which he uninterruptedly punished his fingers, no matter whether he was in company or on his own — or even at concerts, between items! I shall never forget how — only a few minutes after one of his most brilliant triumphs at a concert in the Hall of Nobility — I went to the artist's room with Count Wielhorski to speak with Henselt, and found him, surrounded by the flood-tide of a concert evening, busy with his dumb piano! There was something in this of Hoffman's 'Kreissler' — it was the artist's confession of faith — his way of giving himself up entirely to his art, to the exclusion of everything else. I have often regretted it for his sake, but I have always understood it as a rare faithfulness to conviction, as an extreme of duty to his life-work for art — as a proof of endurance and strength of character such as is peculiar to the Germanic nature. This was not understood by everyone, however — this longing of Henselt's to grasp with his hands the ever receding horizon of ideal perfection!

Also significant in his character is the fact that the mere thought of giving a concert makes him ill! After his first appearance, no amount of persuasion was sufficient to induce him to give another concert — in thirty-three years he gave but three! He was offered payment, in advance, of the highest fee he could reasonably ask, if only he would sit down at the piano and play — but Henselt absolutely refused.

It is quite impossible to induce him to attend a concert given by another — or to visit the opera. He devotes himself entirely to his art, to his pupils, to the Court, to Bach and the Bible. Before Bach comes, however, he still follows his course of physical exercises every evening, forcing, in the sweat of his brow, and in spite of every fatigue, his hands and feet to perform all sorts of complicated evolutions on the horizontal bar! He once got a notion that it was beneficial, and Henselt never changes his opinion. These gymnastics of his have an interesting origin.

In the days of Emperor Nicholas, hygienic gymnastics came into fashion through the performances of a Swedish gymnast whose influence reached the highest social circles. For several winters the Emperor visited, early each morning, the gymnasium in the palace of the Prince of Oldenburg, where he, together with the Grand Duke, the Prince, and the Duke of Leuchenburg, practised their gymnastics. In all this, Henselt, as a friend of royalty, took part. Many years have passed since then, and of all who met there, Henselt alone continues the exercises — a striking example of the persistence of his nature. For the same health reasons, he walks endless distances every day in St. Petersburg, sometimes allowing his carriage to accompany him, but more often preferring to do without it.

Henselt is General-Inspector of the music classes in the royal educational institutions in St. Petersburg and Moscow, which are under the management of the Prince of Oldenburg. On dark winter evenings, Henselt walks quite alone from the Smolna Monastery — one of the largest — through a particularly lonely part of the town back to his house. It is useless to remonstrate with him. We warned him that he might be waylaid. "That would not be easy", was his only answer. "I am agile — I do gymnastics! And I have my preserver", he added, pointing to his stick. So it will always be. A yielding Henselt, at any age, is unimaginable. In these institutions Henselt produces whole generations of well-trained instructresses, thus assuring generations a respectable livelihood for which they have not ceased to be grateful.

Henselt's great Études are to be considered as poems, real "Songs without Words", and he would surely have named them so had this title, brought into vogue by Mendelssohn, not already appeared. The expression *Étude* is not to be understood in this case in the sense of being exercises for piano instruction, as Cramer's are. Everything, of course, is in a sense, a *study* — we shall never finish practising and learning. But these inspirations (Henselt's Études) assume previously finished study — they are in the first rank of the mass of piano literature which has appeared under the title of Études, and which reached its highest point in Chopin.

Henselt's Études are not inferior to those of Chopin, but they present an essentially different emotional realm; they move in a different social sphere, with different forms of intercourse. If we seek to understand these differences, we shall fathom the character of both artist-natures, and discover another criterion for a proper estimate of Henselt.

Henselt, in common with Chopin, acts with direct effect — the effect which speculative, more abstract musical thought does not need, and which is most effective on the piano. He shares with Chopin the peculiar ability of directing the whole power and technique of the instrument to the sense of hearing. Henselt differs from Chopin as the former higher French society of the *salon* differs from German society. During the last few years, Paris has become demoralized — a sort of robber-romance. Even in the days of Louis Philippe, the scene of Dumas' novels was laid in Paris. The Parisian *salon* of those days exists now only in the literature of the time, in its music, in Chopin. Take up a novel of Balzac, and you will find forms of intercourse, relationships, feminine characters and personalities which make up a world apart. It is precisely so with Chopin. It is not so much *what* he says, but how he says it — that is the main point. Whatever seems correct to Parisians, must therefore have universal vitality, and a frivolous conception of the mutual relations of the sexes plays the leading rôle. A more fervent feeling, a deeper conception, is not altogether ruled out, but it disappears under the purple cover under which this very exclusive society seeks to prolong its artistic existence.

On the other hand, take a novel by Auerbach, Spielhagen, or any of the leading German authors. There you will find not such accomplished people as occupy the French scene, and the forms of intercourse may not be so charming; the language will hardly be modelled on the pattern which receive French approval. But the characters will possess a loftier expression of life, and not a purely material point of view depending on the latest fashion. It is just so with Henselt. He reaches his ideal from life itself. Chopin and the French exalt a life justified solely by convention and example, and for this reason recognize therein their own artistic justification! This tendency is unwholesome. However great the charm which its procedure and manners possess, it is, when all is told, a poisoning of the soul with refined poisons. It is the burning by perfumed tapers, when the flame alone is the emblem of real life.

The refined and effeminate character of modern French literature, which is reflected, as it were, in Chopin, finds exceptions in his Polonaises, which are, for him, the higher, more objective form, and his Ballades, which are pictures in small frames (Sonnets — to which his Nocturnes, especially belong). Such exceptions in no way alter the character of the phenomenon as a whole. One can find great depths, and genuine pearls even in Balzac and his imitators. We cannot unconditionally and without reservation classify either phenomenon as higher than the other — we can but discriminate.

Chopin may pass for a lyric epicure. Any depreciative epithets are out of place where a noble spirit, like Chopin, is concerned. He, like Balzac, and all those Parisian exotics, moved in a self-constructed, self imagined *milieu*, yet they still bore the unmistakable mark of genius. Chopin is, with few exceptions, a charming water-colour painter; Henselt paints *al fresco*, even when his subject seems more appropriate to exclude the broader style.

In the difference of their natures, in the irreconcilable divergence between French and German culture, lies the natural reason why Henselt does not play Chopin as that master ought to be played. We can only agree with the great virtuoso that when (as I heard him say) one is a Henselt, one has the right to play as one likes.

We spoke of Henselt's interpretation of Chopin only because the question: "How do you understand Chopin?" is one of the gravest questions one can put to a representative of modern piano playing. In Henselt's interpretation of the Nocturnes and the Mazurkas, I would say (and I speak from personal acquaintance with the composer) that Chopin would have felt as little at home as would a Parisian in the midst of German Society.

Henselt's magnificently powerful manner of playing showed itself to advantage in Chopin's ornamental pieces — which are in Pompeian, not colossal style, and therefore not in keeping with a Titanic conception. In the Mazurkas Henselt allows the *time* to take the leading part. He uses his heavy brush for fullness of tone, where the whole fabric should be delicately woven; his 'rubato' is not the 'rubato' of Chopin. But how I would have enjoyed witnessing Chopin's ecstasy, could he have heard Henselt thunder, whisper, lighten through his A minor Étude (the "Winter Wind"). This rendering of Chopin by Henselt is so poetic, so indescribably grand, so infinitely idealized, as if touched by the wand of Oberon, that I can find no words to adequately describe it. The ineffable tones produced in the right hand to the herculean strokes of the left are like the twinkling of stars — the unknown language of the heights. Taken all in all, this performance of Henselt's is one of the grandest that it has ever been my privilege to hear. From the depths of his soul the artist loves this poem; for years he has fostered and tended it, and warmed it on his breast. When Henselt plays the A minor Étude, he plays it not once, but over and over again, for he cannot satiate himself with the euphony, with whose atmosphere he surrounds himself! If there is any one performance in which the artist's consuming impulse for absolute perfection is realized, I believe it is this — and my opinion is formed by the result of many years of observation.

Two of Henselt's principal compositions are his Concerto in F minor, and the great 'Duo' in one movement, for piano and horn, in B minor. The Concerto is the climax of the most brilliant concert-bravura, together with good musical content. What one might be tempted to regard as mere passage-work, is solid musical thought presented in decorative style. But the execution of this work is so difficult that the artist was never satisfied with his own rendering, and never played the work publicly in St. Petersburg. Neither was he ever quite satisfied with the accompaniment. He often played the Concerto at his own home, and such a colossal subjection of the greatest technical difficulties (difficulties, however, which had a purpose) aroused the greatest musical interest. The 'Duo' too, required a master-pianist to interpret. In my opinion it is the more interesting in this entire literature, as an exponent of pianoforte-bravura in combination with a second instrument. Neither of these works is as widely known as it deserves to be, and this is not caused by the technical difficulties alone. His residence being so far from Germany, and his strong objection to publicity, may have something to do with it, too. Hans von Bülow played the Concerto in St. Petersburg, and thought very highly of it. It is like the apotheosis of the old school in the new era, a task for the well-intended virtuoso-pianist.

When Liszt came to St. Petersburg, he and I and the two Counts Wielhorski visited Henselt. We found the artist waiting for us, and ready to comply with Liszt's particular request that he should play for him. Henselt first gave us his very individual interpretation of Weber's Polacca in E. I watched Liszt. A look of astonishment spread over his face. After Henselt had finished, Liszt said: "I could have had velvet paws too, if I had so wished!" Liszt's approval was so unconditional that when he next visited St. Petersburg and I said to him that Henselt had made great progress, he replied: "Understand, an artist like Henselt does not 'make progress'". It was a reproof — but it was a reproof from Liszt!

Henselt's performance of Weber's Polacca is phenomenal. It combines the greatest power and strength with the greatest tenderness in the interpretation of the poetic thought. From the very first bar with the trill, there arises under Henselt's hands, a vision of a brilliantly lit Valhalla, where kings walk with fair women, and whisper words of love. And then the Trio! Henselt published his own set of variations to this inspired work of a knightly tone-poet, this foremother of Polonaises. These variations are not mere reinforcements. They contain inner parts, more sonorous registers, double passages instead of mere threads, which elevate the piece upon the shield of modern Olympian piano-playing, leaving to the original a certain feeling of tonal emptiness, which, in its time, was fullness of tone. But the thought, the creation, of Weber, still lives immortal. What Henselt has woven into the work, is like the journal of his soul. It is no improvement, no "revised edition", but the homage of our present-day pianist, after fifty years of development, to its emancipator. Henselt's interpretation of Weber, to whom, after all, he stands in closest affinity, is one of his specialities. But Henselt discriminates in Weber. He discriminates between the value of the idea, and its often insufficient or inadequate realization. Hans von Bülow is of the same mind, and Tausig, too, when he made his arrangement of the 'Invitation'. Liszt has just published his arrangement of Weber's piano compositions. At the moment Henselt is occupied with an edition of his own reading of the solo Sonatas — a reading which is the result of a lifetime of careful study, and not the passing fancy of a moment.

Of Weber's Piano Quartet and Trio (with flute), of the E minor Sonata (the fourth), of the Rondo in E flat and the first two Concertos (C and E flat), and of the Variations, Henselt refuses to take any notice. On the other hand, he considers the Sonatas in C, A flat, and D minor, the Clarinet Sonata in E flat, the 'Invitation' (his own arrangement of which appeared long ago in St. Petersburg), the Momento Capriccioso, the Polacca in E, and above all, the Concertstück, the very highest expression of all piano-poetry. His performance of the Concertstück is extraordinary, and if we look at Weber from Henselt's standpoint, it is unapproachable. Henselt throws his own life, his very soul and being into

Weber. He does not play Weber objectively and probably no composer yields more readily to a subjective interpretation than Weber, whose works we understand as redeeming the sensual through the ideal. Weber is love; flirtations, French or other, are foreign to his nature. If it were possible to lose Germany, we should find her again in 'Der Freischütz'. As Weber is 'Der Freischütz', so is he in his piano music. Weber is the last of the Knights. Thus Henselt, his most faithful shield-bearer, interprets him. Henselt's most important interpretation of Weber, are his Polacca in E, the A flat Sonata, the Rondo of the D minor Sonata, where the episode in G, with the trills in the song-like figure in the bass, is expressed in a manner which I would not have believed possible on the piano — it sounded to me like an unspeakably lovely spring-song. These interpretations of Weber culminate in the Concertstück. To hear Henselt play this is an event which will be remembered for ever. He gives it the happiest reading. It takes on quite a different appearance — it seems to prophesy the future of the piano as seen from the date of its composition, in the early twenties. And to think that this subversion of all Hummel's ideas was accomplished by a pupil of Hummel! In order to render the contrast between then and now still more striking, and give the affair a still more fateful appearance, let me add that Henselt has by no means ceased to be a good Hummel pupil. The artist does his best by the well-known Sonatas dedicated to Papa Haydn, the Fantasia in E flat, (Op.18), and the Quintets and Trios by Hummel. Yet these works, compared to those of Weber, are like the toys of childhood. Thus wonderfully is Henselt's nature divided between the doctrines of the good old school, and the acquisitions of the new. He arranged the 'Concertstück' to be played without accompaniment — that is, he so successfully altered the

poem that one does not miss the orchestra, but is
carried away by admiration of the composition. One
example: before the entrance of the March (pianissimo
— the return of the warrior, in the distance), where the
alluring magic of the bassoon and the hushed vibration
of the strings (tremolo) prepare for the *Marcia*, which
stands supreme in the history of music, Henselt
introduces a series of 'volta', short but magnificent
fore-runners of the presto in six-eight time, which are
strikingly effective, and altogether in the spirit of the
situation, for they foreshadow the 'presto' figure — in
which the lady of the castle embraces her returning
lord. Weber himself left us the programme of this piece
in the biography by his son.

Henselt's arrangements for two hands (one should
have at least four to play them) are epoch-making in
"arrangement" literature. There are the three opera
overtures by Weber, together with several of the songs
from 'Oberon', 'Euryanthe,' and 'Freischütz', and the
'Coriolanus' overture of Beethoven. No orchestra
would be able to render the 'Oberon' overture with
such fine nuances, with the flowing, blended harmonies, with the intricate meaning with which Henselt
imbues this instrumental tale. This interpretation is,
indeed, wholly incomparable.

At rare, gracious moments, for his own enjoyment,
Henselt plays the Weber operas four-handed. At these
times, it is easier to be his audience than his partner.
His 'Agathas' and 'Annchens' were better than any that
I ever heard on the stage, and I have heard them all!
What can I say of his Gypsy choruses from 'Preciosa'?
Astounding! — why Henselt never went to the opera
became quite clear. It is Henselt's right *as* a virtuoso to
be thus selective in Weber. For others (and they have
been the gainers thereby) the Piano Quartet, and the
Trio, and the other compositions by Weber which

Henselt rejects, have become life-long friends. Are not the "Sonatas progressives et agréables" (in which the only fault is the French conventional title), arranged for four hands from the too meagre original for piano and violin, operas in disguise? Is not everything comprehended within the bounds of Weber's original 'Pièces' for four hands?

Henselt considered the E flat Clarinet Sonata Weber's greatest work in respect of completeness and unity of design, and he arranged this charming piece for two pianos. On the second he places the clarinet part in his most happy style of accompaniment — a style which no one else could attempt. By this means he obtains a unity and sonorous fullness of tone, and a general effect by which the work is improved a great deal. The artist carries this second part in his heart — he never wrote it down! He also accompanied several of his great Études on a second piano, and in St. Petersburg, he had a second part to the Cramer Études published. The artist considered the Études by Church-Father Cramer, which contrast so strongly with the Weber Muse, such great works of art, that he plays them in St. Petersburg, where his predilection is well known, on two pianos, as fully-fledged concert pieces; and so effective and fully adapted is the secondo to the primo (the original unaltered Étude) that it is hard to think they were ever played otherwise! To us, these productions of Cramer's Études viewed as repertoire pieces, appear as the comments of a philologist on a classic author. From an artistic standpoint, I never enjoyed them. But how old Church-Father Cramer (Beda venerabilis) would have rejoiced to find himself so honoured after a lapse of seventy-five years! How delicately and tastefully Henselt handled them. To invent a second part to the polyphonic compositions of Cramer — always so complete in themselves —

is a problem for the connoisseur. It is a far greater achievement than that of Gounod, who composed a second part to the Bach C major Prelude. Consider the variety of form and rhythm, of expression and conception, contained in the Cramer Études! It was an 'opus desparatum': the thought of producing such a work could have occurred only to a German mind — and only the greatest love for the compositions and the pleasure of solving such a difficult problem could have induced him to attempt it.

On several of the celebrated Moscheles Études (the one in A flat, for instance), Henselt has bestowed the blessing of the modern piano, and paid the greatest compliment to Moscheles by playing these variations to him in Leipzig. I knew Moscheles well. How astounded the neat little man must have been to see Henselt hurl his Achilles spear into the midst of his compositions!

This great German artist, Adolph Henselt, despised ostentation and avoided any kind of publicity, yet he won renown in his fatherland, and I believe these hints of his experiences in a foreign country will — especially to the German reader — form a welcome contribution to the history of the piano of our day. It would require a whole book to give a detailed description of such an important artist as Henselt. Therefore we do not pretend to have exhausted our subject, and I can but assure the friendly reader that, to the best of our ability, we have endeavoured to draw in outline (as the English say) one of the most remarkable phenomena of this century. In closing, let us glance for a moment at the outward appearance of the artist, which is more often than one might think, mistaken for an exponent of the inner man.

When Henselt first came to St. Petersburg, he was the perfect example of the German youth — the

Germanic hero, confident of success, without foreign polish. There was a suggestion of Siegfried in his character; one could read something of the Nibelungen in his deep, expressive eyes. Throughout Germany one may find portraits of the artist taken at this period. In one especially, he is taken full face — he looks you frankly in the eyes and you discern the romantic trait which is prominent in his character — the never satisfied soul, continually striving to reach the ideal of ultimate perfection.

Henselt is an ego, a distinct personality. Like Liszt and Chopin, he is the fountain head of a current, a tendency, on the pianoforte, and his own ancestor. To imitate Henselt's performance is impossible, because it is specifically individual. For this reason alone Henselt has no successor. The best of his pupils in Russia, though true virtuosos, reproduce only his material side, not his heart, which remains his own, inseparable from his total personality.

If anyone ever approached Weber at the piano, it is Henselt. He, like Weber, is a spirit — a cosmos of ideas, such as one can find only in the ages of the organic life at a time when people had leisure for contemplation and possessed greater power of thought and feeling than in our day. It is difficult, now, to believe that such a time ever existed!

It is not only in the fruitful treatment of the piano that Henselt resembles Weber; it is not in the tenths, and the chord stretches, from which Henselt, like Weber, reaps advantage. It is in the spirit, influencing the soul from the German soul, and not from speculative musical ideas. It is the life of the German heart, which is sufficient unto itself and courts nothing foreign. As the romantic poet has it:

Überwunden von der Schönheit,
Will ich ewig nach dir ziehen.*

Henselt's nature suggests an indestructible youthfulness. Such a nature cannot grow old — it must be, and
remain, like itself alone. In Germany one may see,
among grey-haired statesmen, a similar youthfulness of
thought. With them it is the legacy of the German
academic life, but with our artist it is the German soul.

In dem die Welt sich,
Die Ewige spiegelt!**

* Overwhelmed by the beauty I am eternally drawn to you.
** In this the world is eternally reflected.